THE FBAR GUIDE BOOK

The Complete FBAR Compliance Guide

The FBAR Guide Book

By: Mr. Anthony N. Verni

ISBN: 978-93-5605-586-5

First Edition

Understanding the FBAR filing requirements is crucial for anyone who may have foreign bank accounts, whether they are expatriates living abroad, citizens traveling internationally, or businesses engaged in global transactions. The rules surrounding the FBAR are not only intricate but also fraught with significant penalties for non-compliance, making it vital for filers to fully grasp their obligations.

Anthony N.Verni

LEGAL DISCLOSURES

No Attorney-Client Relationship or Legal Advice

The content of this book has been prepared by Anthony N.Verni for informational purposes only and does not constitute any legal advice. The information in this book shall not be construed as an offer to represent you, nor is it intended to create, nor shall the receipt of such information constitute, an attorney-client relationship. I hope that you will find the information useful, and I would be delighted to speak with you to answer any questions you may have about my office.

Readers should not act upon the information contained in this book, or decide not to act based upon the information contained in this book, without seeking appropriate professional counsel from an attorney licensed in the user's jurisdiction to advise appropriately.

Intellectual Property Policy

This book, the name Anthony N. Verni, and the logos used in this book are the property of The Law Office of Anthony N. Verni, Inc. and are protected by the intellectual property laws of the United States. You may make a copy of the materials in this book for your own personal, noncommercial use, but you may not make or distribute copies of any part of this website for any other purpose.

IRS Circular 230 Notice

In accordance with IRS requirements, this is to inform you that any information contained in this book that could be construed as U.S. tax advice is not written or intended to be used, and cannot be used, for the following:

(i) Avoiding penalties under the Internal Revenue Code or,

(ii) Promoting, marketing, or recommending to another party any transaction or matter addressed on this website.

About the Author

Anthony is an attorney and certified public accountant with over 25 years of experience practising before the Internal Revenue Service, United States Tax Court, and United States District Court. He has represented clients in domestic and international tax controversy cases, including examinations and appeals, as well as before the United States Tax Court. As part of his practice, Anthony has prepared thousands of income tax returns and also assisted clients with related compliance work.

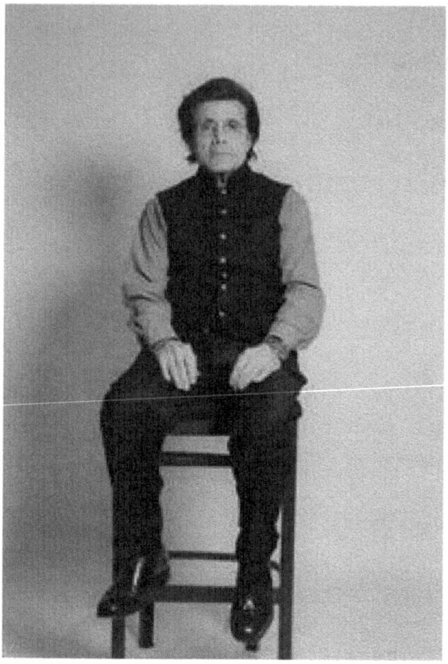

Anthony represents expatriates and other U.S. taxpayers who have failed to report income from their offshore accounts or other foreign sources, as well as taxpayers who have failed to report their interest in or signatory authority over Foreign Financial Accounts **('FFA')** and individuals who have failed to report their Foreign Financial Assets under the Foreign Asset Tax Compliance Act **('FATCA')**. Anthony has assisted clients from all over the world with participation under the Voluntary Disclosure Practice Rules, has assisted clients in making disclosures of their foreign assets under the Foreign and Domestic Streamline Procedures, and has also assisted clients with other tax and financial reporting compliance issues.

Introduction

Financial transparency has become a cornerstone of international regulatory compliance in an increasingly interconnected world. At the heart of this movement in the United States lies the Report of Foreign Bank and Financial Accounts (FBAR), a critical reporting requirement that U.S. persons must adhere to when holding accounts in foreign financial institutions. The FBAR is an essential tool for the U.S. government to combat tax evasion, money laundering, and other illicit financial activities. However, the complexities surrounding FBAR filing can be daunting for many individuals and entities.

Understanding the FBAR filing requirements is crucial for anyone with foreign bank accounts, whether they are expatriates living abroad, citizens traveling internationally, or businesses engaged in global transactions. The rules surrounding the FBAR are not only intricate but also fraught with significant penalties for non-compliance, making it vital for filers to grasp their obligations fully.

31 U.S.C. §5314 requires U.S. citizens and permanent residents of the United States to file a report. The FBAR implementing regulations provide that a *"U.S. Person*

Rwho has a financial interest in or signature or other authority over a bank, securities or other financial account in another country" is required to file an FBAR *"for any year in which the aggregate balance for such foreign financial Raccount or accounts exceeds $10,000 at any time during the calendar year"* 31 C.F.R. §1010.350(a), and 31 C.F.R. §1010.306(c)(2011).

31 U.S.C. §5321(a)(2) authorises the Secretary of the Treasury to impose penalties for failure to file an FBAR report. The relevant FBAR penalty provisions include a $10,000 Penalty under Section 5321(a)(5)(B) for non-willful violations (the "Non-Willful FBAR Penalty"), which may be excused where "reasonable cause" can be established, as well as a Willful FBAR Penalty for willful violations. The willful FBAR penalty under Section 5321(a)(5)(C) is the greater of $100,000 or 50% of the amount of the "transaction" or, in cases where no FBAR is filed, the balance in the account at the time of the violation.

People who fail or refuse to file their FBARS and/or those who fail or refuse to report the income derived from their Foreign Financial Accounts ("FFAs") may feel that the Government has overlooked them. Those who have hidden their foreign assets by placing them in the name of a nominee, shell company, or some other entity may, likewise, now feel they are safe. Think Again.

Prior to the termination of the Offshore Voluntary Disclosure Program ('OVDP') in September of 2018, at-risk taxpayers sought protection from criminal prosecution by entering into the OVDP. Some OVDP participants deliberately omitted large account balance FFAs from their FBAR filings in order to reduce the Miscellaneous Offshore Penalty. Others elected to "opt out" of the OVDP in hopes of either no penalty or paying the less onerous Non-Willful FBAR Penalty.

With the introduction of the Voluntary Disclosure Practice Rules (VDP) in November of 2018, taxpayers face even more scrutiny, in part, because they are now required to admit that their compliance failures were due to willful conduct. The result of such admissions could result in criminal prosecution in addition to the willful civil and criminal FBAR penalties.

There were also those who may have attempted to game the system by foregoing the use of the VDP, the OVDP, or its prior iterations, and instead utilizing one of the two streamlined procedures as a means of avoiding the costly willful civil FBAR penalty, associated legal costs, and possible criminal prosecution.

Taxpayers who intentionally omitted FFAs with significant balances have been subject to the willful FBAR penalty and, in some cases, have also been prosecuted. Some U.S. taxpayers who opted out of the OVDP, have been successful in reducing or avoiding any FBAR Penalty. However, others have not been as fortunate and consequently have been subject to the willful FBAR Penalty in amounts far in excess of the Miscellaneous Offshore Penalty they would have paid had they remained in the OVDP.

The catalyst for change started in 2008 when the DOJ prosecuted Swiss UBS, as well as a number of its advisors, attorneys, and financial professionals, for assisting U.S. taxpayers in hiding foreign assets and income from the IRS. To avoid prosecution, UBS and the U.S. Government entered into a *deferred prosecution agreement* wherein UBS was, among other things, required to pay stiff penalties and admit that its cross-border banking practices made use of Swiss privacy laws to aid and assist U.S. taxpayers in committing offshore tax evasion. As part of the deal, UBS also agreed to take affirmative steps to improve transparency and to provide the U.S. Government with information on its U.S. account holders.

Since the UBS case and the DOJ's establishment of the *Swiss Bank Program*, many FFIs have been subject to prosecution and have entered into either DPAs or non-prosecution agreements. These institutions have also been required to pay large penalties, agree to compliance reforms, and have had to provide information on their U.S. account holders. Even small FFIs that rely on correspondents.

While the U.S. assault on international banking practices and U.S. account holders over the past fifteen years has motivated some U.S. customers to come out of the dark and disclose their foreign assets and income, some taxpayers persist in holding out and are actively engaged in unlawful practices designed to avoid detection by the IRS.

Other U.S. account holders have scrambled to close existing accounts at one FFI and transferred the proceeds or assets to another. In some instances, the move entails transferring an existing account in one country to an FFI in another. Still others have elected to form multiple entities as a means of making detection more difficult.

Table of Contents

Chapter 1

Understanding the Basics of the Report of Foreign Bank and Financial Accounts

With the advent of globalization, individuals and businesses often engage in financial transactions that cross international borders.

This cross-border movement of money presents numerous advantages, such as enhanced investment opportunities and diversified portfolios. However, it also brings a heightened responsibility for taxpayers to maintain compliance through financial reporting, particularly those set forth by the U.S. Department of the Treasury. One such report is the Report of Foreign Bank and Financial Accounts, commonly referred to as the "FBAR".

The FBAR is a crucial reporting requirement for U.S. citizens, residents, and any entities with a financial interest in or signature authority over one or more foreign financial accounts. Established under the Bank Secrecy Act, the FBAR mandates individuals to disclose certain accounts outside the United States. This requirement is aimed at combating tax evasion and money laundering, as well as promoting transparency in international banking activities.

The primary requirement for filing an FBAR is to meet certain thresholds concerning the total value of foreign financial accounts. If the aggregate value of these accounts exceeds $10,000 at any point during the calendar year, a "U.S. Person" is compelled to file an FBAR. This threshold applies to all foreign financial accounts, including bank accounts, mutual funds, trusts, and other similar financial instruments.

It's worth noting that the obligation to file an FBAR is broad, encompassing not only individual U.S. citizens but also residents, partnerships, corporations, and limited liability companies. Consequently, many individuals and entities engaged in international financial activities need to be mindful of this requirement to avoid severe penalties.

Not all foreign financial accounts require reporting. To fall under the purview of the FBAR, the accounts must be "foreign," meaning they are located outside the United States. Common examples of reportable accounts include Bank Accounts, including savings, checking, and time deposit accounts held at foreign banks.

1.1 Investment Accounts

- Brokerage accounts that allow for purchasing foreign stocks, bonds, or other securities;
- Mutual Funds registered outside the U.S., whether publicly traded or privately held;
- A corporation, partnership, or limited liability company;
- Trusts & Estates: Foreign trusts or estates managed from abroad that fall under the financial account definitions.

However, certain accounts are exempt from FBAR reporting. This includes accounts maintained within certain foreign entities or accounts that are owned by a governmental entity or international organizations.

Filing an FBAR involves submitting Form FinCEN 114 online through the Financial Crimes Enforcement Network (FinCEN) portal. It is important to note that this form is separate from the taxpayer's annual income tax return and must be filed electronically by April 15 of the following year, with an automatic extension available until October 15. In addition, filers should be aware that the FBAR has no associated filing fee, unlike many other tax-related forms. The form itself requires information such as personal identification details, a description of the account(s), the Nname and address of the financial institution, and the maximum value of the accounts during the reporting period. Accuracy and completeness are paramount, as the consequences for failing to file, filing late, or inaccurately can be severe, ranging from monetary penalties to criminal charges.

The penalties for failing to file an FBAR can be staggeringly high. The U.S. government categorizes these penalties into non-willful and willful violations. Non-willful violations may incur fines of up to $10,000 per violation, while willful violations can lead to penalties of the greater of $100,000 or 50% of the account balance at the time of the violation.

Furthermore, failure to comply with FBAR reporting requirements can also trigger scrutiny from the Internal Revenue Service (IRS) and potentially lead to broader tax compliance issues, including criminal penalties and possible incarceration. As such, anyone subject to these rules must approach reporting with diligence and care. The Report of Foreign Bank and Financial

Accounts is a crucial tool in the United States' efforts to combat money laundering, tax evasion, and other financial crimes. This chapter explores the significance of FBAR compliance both for individuals and the broader context of the U.S. financial system. Understanding these implications is essential for anyone with foreign financial accounts, whether they are individuals, businesses, or financial institutions.

The FBAR reporting requirements were enacted as part of the Bank Secrecy Act of 1970, a legislative response to the growing concerns about financial crime and the need for more stringent measures to ensure transparency in financial transactions. Over the years, amendments and regulations have expanded the scope of reporting, particularly following the 2008 financial crisis, which underscored vulnerabilities in both the domestic and international financial systems. The increasing globalization of commerce has made FBAR compliance not only a regulatory obligation but also a critical element of financial responsibility.

For U.S. Persons, including citizens, residents, and entities, FBAR compliance is not optional. The requirement to file is triggered when the aggregate value of foreign financial accounts exceeds $10,000 at any time during the calendar year. Late or non-compliance can lead to severe penalties, including substantial fines and criminal charges in extreme cases. Understanding these legal obligations is paramount for individuals and businesses who want to maintain their good standing and avoid unnecessary legal repercussions.

The penalties for failing to comply with FBAR regulations

can be severe. Non-willful violations may incur a fine of up to $10,000 per violation, while willful violations can attract penalties reaching $100,000 or 50% of the account balance, whichever is higher. Such financial repercussions can severely impede an individual's or a business's financial plans and stability. It can also resolve themselves from these substantial penalties while promoting a culture of compliance within their financial dealings.

FBAR compliance plays an integral role in maintaining the integrity of the global financial system. By ensuring that foreign-held assets are properly reported, the U.S. government can identify illicit financial activity and enforce tax compliance effectively. This transparency not in financial chaos, damage to reputation, and the breakup of a family.

By ensuring timely and accurate FBAR filings, individuals can safeguard thet only combats tax evasion but also promotes fair competition among businesses, leveling the playing field for those who operate honestly within the legal frameworks established by their respective jurisdictions.

Furthermore, the U.S. compliance with international financial reporting standards strengthens relationships with foreign governments and aids international cooperation in fighting financial crime. Ensuring funds are not funnelled into illicit activities contributes positively to global economic stability.

On a more personal level, FBAR compliance can instill a sense of discipline and awareness regarding one's financial affairs. Regularly tracking foreign accounts and maintaining clear records can enhance an individual's overall financial literacy. Individuals who engage with financial regulatory requirements often find they are better equipped to manage their assets, plan their finances, and even navigate investment opportunities abroad.

Moreover, the act of reporting foreign accounts can highlight areas of financial risk that individuals may not have previously considered. By fostering awareness through compliance, individuals are encouraged to take a proactive approach to their personal finance management.

For financial institutions, strict compliance with FBAR regulations fosters a culture of transparency and trust. Customers and clients are more likely to feel secure about their financial dealings when they know institutions adhere to stringent laws and best practices. As compliance becomes an integral part of an institution's operations, it enhances the reputation of both the institution and the broader financial ecosystem.

Moreover, institutions that facilitate foreign transactions or maintain accounts for clients must prioritize FBAR compliance not only to avoid legal penalties but also to attract and retain clients who value integrity and transparency in their financial dealings.

The Report of Foreign Bank and Financial Accounts is a critical component of U.S. tax compliance for citizens, residents, and entities with foreign financial interests. The FBAR process ensures that the U.S. government is informed about its taxpayers' foreign accounts and assets, which helps combat tax evasion and maintain the integrity of the financial system. This chapter provides a comprehensive overview of the FBAR process, detailing its significance, requirements, and the steps necessary to comply with the relevant regulations.

The Report of Foreign Bank and Financial Accounts, known as FinCEN Form 114, is a form that U.S. persons must file annually if they have foreign financial accounts that exceed a certain threshold. The primary purpose of FBAR is to provide the U.S. Department of the Treasury with information about foreign bank accounts, helping to detect and deter money laundering, tax evasion, and other financial crimes.

The FBAR requirement is established under the BSA, specifically Section 5314, and is enforced by the Financial Crimes Enforcement Network (FinCEN). U.S. persons must adhere to these regulations to avoid significant penalties, including substantial fines for non-compliance.

The term "U.S. Person" includes:

- U.S. citizens;
- U.S. residents (including Green Card holders);
- Domestic entities, such as corporations, partnerships, and trusts.

A U.S. person must file an FBAR if the aggregate value of their foreign financial accounts exceeds $10,000 at any point during the calendar year. This threshold applies to all foreign accounts combined, regardless of whether each account meets the threshold on its own.

The FBAR reporting requirement includes a wide range of

foreign accounts, such as:

- Bank accounts;
- Securities accounts;
- Mutual funds;
- Insurance sub-accounts with cash value.

However, it does not include foreign real estate, foreign currency accounts outside of a conventional bank account, or accounts owned by foreign entities.

Taxpayers should first assess whether they have a filing requirement based on the ownership and value of their foreign accounts. Determining the maximum value of all foreign financial accounts throughout the calendar year is vital for compliance.

To successfully file the FBAR, individuals must collect necessary information about each foreign financial account, including:

- The account number;
- The name and address of the foreign financial institution;
- The type of account;
- The highest balance during the year.

The FBAR is filed electronically through FinCEN's BSA E-filing System. Taxpayers must provide all required information accurately and completely. To avoid discrepancies, it is also important to ensure that the information matches the records from the foreign banks.

The FBAR submission deadline is April 15 of the following year, with an automatic extension available until October 15.

However, extensions only apply to individual tax return filings and do not extend the FBAR deadline itself, making timely filing crucial.

After submission, it is essential to maintain copies of the filed FBAR and supporting documents for at least five years from the date of filing. This documentation may be needed for future audits or inquiries by tax authorities.

The FBAR process includes strict penalties for those who fail to file or report their foreign accounts. Non-compliance can result in civil penalties, which can amount to $10,000 per violation for non-willful violations. In cases of willful violations, the penalties can escalate to the greater of $100,000 or 50% of the account's highest value. Knowing and adhering to FBAR requirements is critical to avoiding these severe consequences.

The Report of Foreign Bank and Financial Accounts (FBAR), reported on FinCEN Form 114, is a critical compliance obligation for U.S. persons with foreign financial accounts. Given its importance in combating tax evasion and improving transparency in international finance, the FBAR has become a subject of misconceptions. The purpose of the following chapters is to clarify some of the most common misunderstandings surrounding the FBAR and to provide a clear and accurate picture of what it entails and its implications for U.S. taxpayers.

One of the most pervasive misconceptions is that only U.S. citizens living abroad or expatriates must file the FBAR. In reality, any U.S. person, including citizens, residents, and entities (such as corporations and partnerships), with a financial interest in or signature authority over foreign financial accounts totaling $10,000 or more at any time during the calendar year is required to file. This means that even U.S. citizens living domestically who have overseas banking accounts must comply with FBAR requirements.

Another common error is equating FBAR filing with regular tax returns. While they both fall under U.S. federal regulations, they serve distinct purposes. The FBAR is focused specifically on reporting foreign accounts and does not include information about income generated from those accounts, which is reported on the taxpayer's annual tax return (Form 1040). Failing to recognize this difference can lead to serious penalties for non-compliance.

Some believe the FBAR requirement applies solely to accounts with a balance exceeding $10,000. However, the filing requirement kicks in as soon as the aggregate balances of all foreign accounts exceed this threshold at any point during the calendar year, not only at year-end. Therefore, if a taxpayer has multiple foreign accounts whose combined total surpasses $10,000, even if each account holds less, an FBAR must be filed.

A frequent misunderstanding is the assumption that FBAR filings are only required on an annual basis. While it is correct that the FBAR is typically filed annually, the due date can vary, especially if the taxpayer has not filed previously or if there are significant changes in account ownership. Furthermore, in situations such as the declaration of a new account or a substantial change in financial status, an FBAR may need to be filed sooner.

Some taxpayers regularly file income tax returns and

include Form 8938. By doing so, they conclude there is no need to file an FBAR since the financial accounts have been included on Form 8938.

In addition, some taxpayers discount the importance of making a return disclosure on Schedule B. Some are so bold that they will respond "no" to questions 7(a) and 7(b) on Schedule B, Part III. (Remember that a taxpayer signs a tax return under penalties of perjury.) Whether the failure to make a disclosure is an innocent one or whether a taxpayer responds "no" to the 7(a) and 7(b) questions, in either case, these choices may serve as a bar to any defence that the taxpayer's conduct was non-willful.

Many taxpayers are unaware that the penalties for failing to file an FBAR can be severe. The IRS imposes penalties for non-willful and willful violations, with the latter facing much more significant fines. Non-willful violations can result in fines of up to $10,000 per reportviolation, while willful violations can lead to penalties ranging from $100,000 or 50% of the account balance during the violation. In extreme cases, criminal charges can be brought against individuals who intentionally fail to report their foreign accounts.

While both the FBAR and the Foreign Account Tax Compliance Act (FATCA) pertain to foreign accounts, they are not interchangeable. FBAR focuses on reporting foreign financial accounts and does not require a taxpayer to declare the income generated, while FATCA requires U.S. taxpayers to store portfolio-specified foreign financial assets on Form 8938 as part of their annual tax return, including income generated from those assets. Understanding the distinctions between these two requirements is crucial for compliance.

Some taxpayers mistakenly believe they can submit their FBAR at the same time as their annual tax returns. However, the FBAR has a different submission process and deadline. While tax returns are typically due on April 15, the FBAR is due on April 15 as well, but provides an automatic extension till October 15 if requested. Not ensuring timely and separate submissions can lead to complications and missed deadlines.

Lastly, individuals often misunderstand which accounts must be reported. While most foreign bank accounts are subject to reporting, certain accounts may be exempt, such as accounts maintained at a U.S. military banking facility or accounts owned by the taxpayer but held in a foreign country by a foreign branch of a U.S. bank. Taxpayers must conduct thorough research to ensure they're fully compliant with reporting requirements.

The FBAR is an increasingly vital component of U.S. tax compliance for individuals with foreign financial interests. Understanding these common misconceptions can help U.S. taxpayers navigate the complexities surrounding the FBAR and ensure compliance, thus avoiding potential penalties and legal issues. As international banking practices evolve, taxpayers must educate themselves and seek guidance from tax professionals to navigate the intricacies of FBAR requirements effectively. Ultimately, awareness and understanding are the best tools in ensuring compliance and safeguarding financial interests when dealing with foreign accounts.

By prioritizing FBAR compliance, individuals can protect themselves from legal risks, contribute to the integrity of the financial system, and enhance their financial management practices. In doing so, they play a vital role in fostering trust in a complex and interconnected global economy. The importance of FBAR compliance cannot be overstated; it is a cornerstone of responsible financial behavior in an increasingly globalized world.

Chapter 2

The Evolution of FBAR: Historical Context and Legal Framework

The Bank Secrecy Act

On October 26, 1970, Congress enacted the Bank Secrecy Act (BSA), also known as the "Currency and Foreign Transaction Reports", to address the legal and economic impact of foreign banking in the United States. The BSA was enacted, in part, based upon the findings by the House Committee on Banking and Currency (the "Committee"). Following a one-day investigative hearing held on December 9, 1968, the committee concluded that Americans were using secret foreign bank accounts and foreign financial institutions for nefarious purposes, including income tax evasion, money laundering, and other crimes.

As part of the BSA, Congress tasked the Treasury Secretary with the responsibility of promulgating regulations designed to facilitate the implementation of the BSA. As part of the implementation of the BSA, 31 C.F.R. §103.27 requires a U.S. citizen with an interest in or control over one or more foreign financial accounts with a value exceeding $10,000 at any time during that calendar year to file FinCen Form 114 (previously TDF 90-22.1) with the Commissioner of Internal Revenue on or before June 30 of the following year. Although the power to assess a civil monetary penalty for FBAR violations was initially vested with the Treasury Secretary, it was later delegated to the Financial Crimes

Enforcement Network (FinCEN). *Treasury Order 180-01, 67 Fed. Reg. 64697 (2002)*. Authority was once again delegated to the Internal Revenue Service. 31 C.F.R. §103.57.

Prior to 2004, the BSA permitted the imposition of an FBAR penalty only for willful violations of §5314. The penalty for willful violations prior to 2004 was capped at the greater of $25,000 or $100,000 under *§5321(a)(5)(B)*. Enforcement of *§5321(a)(5)(B)(i)* is mirrored in the regulations under *31 CFR 103.57(g)(2)*. Although §5314 is silent on assessing a negligence penalty, the regulations permitted the assessment of a negligence penalty not to exceed $500.00. 31 CFR 103.57(h).

The civil FBAR penalty structure was amended in 2004 as part of the AJCA to include a maximum penalty of $10,000 for any violation of the provisions of *§5314*. In addition, the penalty for willful FBAR violations previously provided for in *§5321(a)(5)(B)* was increased under *§5321(a)(5)(C)(i),* a newly created provision, to the greater of $100,000 or 50% of the account balance. The legislative history related to the changes to the willful FBAR penalty chronicles Congressional concern over the lack of compliance in financial reporting related to offshore accounts. Congress made clear that improved compliance was the impetus behind raising the maximum penalty for willful FBAR violations.

Congress also created a separate provision for a civil penalty for non-willful violations, making a clear distinction between willful and non-willful violations. H.R. Rep 108-755 at 615 (2004) (Conf. Rep.).

The power to assess a civil monetary penalty for FBAR

violations was vested with the Treasury Secretary but later delegated to the Financial Crimes Enforcement Network (Treasury Order 180-01, 67 Fed. Reg 64697 (2002). Authority was once again delegated to the Internal Revenue Service under 31 C.F.R. *§103.57.*

The original purpose of the Bank Secrecy Act, which included Section 5314, was to require certain reports and records that have a high degree of usefulness to the U.S. government in carrying out criminal, taxable, or regulatory investigations. The purpose of the Bank Secrecy Act was subsequently broadened in 2001 with the passage of the Patriot Act. As part of the legislation, Congress inserted language clarifying that the FBAR was also useful in conducting activities to protect against international terrorism. Along with expanding the scope of the law, the Patriot Act required the Secretary to study methods for improving compliance with Section 5314 and submit annual reports to Congress regarding his progress. "The Evolution of the FBAR: "Where we were, where we are, and why it matters."

31 U.S.C. §5314 req*uires* U.S. citizens and permanent residents of the United States to file a "*report.*" The FBAR implementing regulations provide that a *"U.S Person who has a financial interest in or signature or other authority over a bank, securities, or other financial account in another country"* is required to file an FBAR *"for any year in which the aggregate balance for such foreign financial account or accounts exceeds $10,000 at any time during the calendar year" (*See *31 C.F.R. §1010.350(a)* and *31 C.F.R. §1010.306(c) (2011).)*

31 U.S.C. §5321(a)(2) authorizes the Secretary of the

Treasury to impose penalties for failure to file an FBAR report. The relevant FBAR penalty provisions include a $10,000 Penalty under *Section 5321(a)(5)(B)* for non-willful violations (the "non-willful FBAR penalty"), which may be excused where "reasonable cause" can be established, as well as a willful FBAR penalty for willful violations. The Willful FBAR Penalty under *Section 5321(a)(5)©* is the greater of $100,000 or 50% of the amount of the "transaction" or, in cases where no FBAR is filed, the balance in the account at the time of the violation.

Regulations and Guidelines: Introduction to Title 31

Title 31 of the United States Code is a comprehensive framework of statutes and regulations governing the financial systems of the United States. It encompasses various topics, including monetary transactions, anti-money laundering measures (AMI), and the reporting requirements for financial institutions. The primary objective of Title 31 is to safeguard the integrity of the financial system, ensure the reporting of suspicious activities, and facilitate the government's efforts in combating any financial crimes.

This chapter aims to provide an overview of the key regulations and guidelines under Title 31, focusing on the importance of compliance, the roles of various entities, and the implications of failing to adhere to regulations.

Key Components of Title 31

Here are the key components of the Title 31.

Anti-Money Laundering Regulations

One of the core components of Title 31 is its anti-money laundering framework. Financial institutions are mandated to implement robust AML programs that include customer due diligence (CDD), suspicious activity reporting (SAR), and record-keeping requirements. These regulations are designed to detect and deter the financial transactions that may facilitate criminal activities and terrorism financing.

Customer Due Diligence (CDD)

Financial institutions must establish the identity of their customers and understand the nature of their business activities. This begins with the collection of identifying information and risk assessment. Institutions are required to monitor transactions and recognize patterns that may indicate money laundering activities.

Suspicious Activity Reporting (SAR)

When financial institutions observe suspicious behavior or transactions that may violate federal laws, they are required to file an SAR with the Financial Crimes Enforcement Network (FinCEN). The guidelines stipulate the circumstances under which a port must be filed, the information that must be included, and the timelines for reporting.

Currency Transaction Reporting

Title 31 also mandates the reporting of certain cash transactions. Financial institutions must report transactions exceeding $10,000 in a single day to FinCEN. This regulation plays a critical role in tracking large cash movements that could indicate illicit activities.

Recordkeeping Requirements

To support the reporting of suspicious activities and currency transactions, Title 31 sets forth specific recordkeeping requirements. Financial institutions must maintain detailed records of all transactions, customer identification information, and SAR filings. These records must be kept for a minimum of five years and must be readily available for examinations by regulatory authorities.

Compliance Obligations

Compliance with Title 31 is not merely a regulatory requirement; it is integral to the operational integrity of financial institutions. Organizations must establish strong compliance programs, conduct regular employee training, and perform independent audits to ensure adherence to Title 31 regulations.

Training and Awareness

Staff training is crucial for ensuring that employees understand their responsibilities under Title 31. Training programs should cover the recognition of suspicious activities, the procedures for filing SARs, and the importance of customer due diligence. Regular updates and refresher courses should be part of the compliance strategy to keep employees informed of any regulatory changes.

Internal Controls and Auditing

Financial institutions must implement effective internal controls to monitor compliance with Title 31 regulations. This includes conducting independent audits to evaluate the effectiveness of the AML program, reviewing the adequacy of reported suspicious activities, and ensuring that proper recordkeeping practices are followed.

Consequences of Non-Compliance

The failure to comply with Title 31 regulations can result in severe consequences for financial institutions. These may include hefty fines, legal repercussions, and reputational damage. Regulatory agencies, including FinCEN and the Office of Foreign Assets Control (OFAC), can impose penalties that can severely affect a company's operations.

Civil and Criminal Penalties

Non-compliance can lead to both civil and criminal penalties. Civil penalties can include monetary fines, while criminal penalties can result in imprisonment for individuals if found guilty of willful violations of Title 31 regulations. The severity of the punishment often correlates with the extent of the violations and whether the institution took steps to remedy the issues.

Reputational Damage

In addition to financial repercussions, failing to comply with Title 31 regulations can irreparably damage an institution's reputation. Clients and partners may seek to distance themselves from organizations perceived as noncompliant, leading to loss of business and diminished stakeholder trust.

Title 31 regulations and guidelines are the critical components of the U.S. financial regulatory framework. They serve as essential tools in the fight against financial crimes, promoting transparency, accountability, and trust in the financial system. Understanding and implementing these regulations is a fundamental responsibility for financial institutions seeking to operate within the law and maintain their reputations.

In a constantly evolving regulatory landscape, vigilance and proactive compliance strategies are key to protecting institutions from the risks associated with failure to comply with Title 31. Continuous education, regular assessments, and a culture of compliance within organizations are vital to ensuring adherence to these important regulations. As financial crime methods evolve, so must the strategies financial institutions employ to mitigate risks and uphold the integrity of the financial system.

Chapter 3

Understanding the FBAR Filing Criteria

FBAR is required if all of the following are present.

- The filer is a U.S. person;
- The U.S. person has a financial account(s);
- The financial account is in a foreign country;
- The U.S. person has a financial interest in the account, or signature, or other authority over the foreign financial account;
- The aggregate amount(s) in the account(s) valued in dollars exceed $10,000 at any time during the calendar year.

Definition of "U.S. Person" for FBAR Purposes

In the realm of U.S. taxation and foreign financial disclosures, understanding the definition of a "U.S. Person" is critical, particularly in relation to the Report of Foreign Bank and Financial Accounts (FBAR) requirements. The FBAR is a key compliance tool used by the Financial Crimes Enforcement Network (FinCEN) to combat tax evasion and to monitor foreign accounts that U.S. citizens and residents hold. In order to fully grasp the implications of these regulations, one must first understand who qualifies as a U.S. person for these purposes.

Legal Framework

The term "U.S. Person" is defined by the Bank Secrecy Act (BSA) of 1970, along with subsequent regulations issued by the

U.S. Treasury. According to the regulations, the following categories are included in the definition of "U.S. Person" for FBAR purposes:

- **3.2.1.1:** A U.S. person is defined by reference to three sources. 31 U.S.C.5314 and 31 C.F.R.103.24 identify persons who may be subject to the FBAR reporting requirement. The FBAR instructions identify a smaller group of persons who must file FBARs than could have been required, under the statute and regulations, to file.
- **3.2.1.1:** A citizen of the United States has a U.S. birth certificate or naturalization papers.
- **3.2.1.1:** A "resident" of the United States is a permanent resident. "Permanent resident" is not defined in *the FBAR instructions, regulations, or statute. The definition of "resident alien" found in IRC§7701(b)* is not applicable for FBAR purposes. The plain meaning of the term "resident" (in this context, someone living in the U.S. and not planning to leave the U.S. permanently) should be used for FBAR examination purposes. Although IRC *§7701(b)* is not applicable, an individual can establish that he is not a resident for FBAR purposes if he can show that none of the following three criteria apply:
    - ➔ **3.2.1.4:** For FBAR purposes, the definition of "person" also includes a corporation, trust, or partnership.
    - ➔ **3.2.1.4:** A corporation that owns directly or indirectly more than a 50% interest in one or more other entities is permitted to file a consolidated FBAR, on behalf of

itself and the other entities. The consolidated report must include a list of the entities. An authorized official of the parent corporation should sign the consolidated report.

Implications of Being a U.S. Person

Understanding the classification of "U.S. Person" is vital due to the reporting obligations accompanying this designation. U.S. Persons are required to report any foreign bank accounts or other financial accounts in which they have a financial interest or signatory authority if the aggregate value of these accounts exceeds $10,000 at any time during the calendar year. This requirement is strictly enforced, and non-compliance can lead to severe penalties, including fines and potential criminal charges.

Exemptions and Special Considerations

While the definition of U.S. Person is straightforward, there are exceptions and nuances one should consider:

- **3.4.1:** Dual Citizens: Individuals holding dual citizenship may encounter additional complexities when dealing with FBAR requirements, as they have obligations in both jurisdictions.

U.S. Persons Living Abroad

Many U.S. citizens or residents living overseas may hold foreign accounts and still be subject to FBAR compliance, even if they aren't physically present in the U.S. during the reporting period.

Trusts and Estates

The requirements can also be complex when it comes to trusts and estates, as the classification of U.S. Persons can depend on various factors, including the residency status of trustees and grantors.

Distinguishing the Term "U.S. Person" under Title 31 and Title 26

Understanding the term "U.S. Person" is crucial for individuals navigating their tax obligations and financial reporting requirements in the United States. This chapter aims to elucidate the differences between the definition of a 'U.S. Person' in the context of the Report of Foreign Bank and Financial Accounts (FBAR) under Title 31 and for income tax purposes under Title 26. Recognizing these distinctions can help taxpayers avoid common pitfalls and ensure compliance with both the Bank Secrecy Act and the Internal Revenue Code (IRC).

Defining "U.S. Person" for FBAR Purposes

The term "U.S. Person" as it relates to the FBAR filing, is defined under the Bank Secrecy Act (BSA). According to the Financial Crimes Enforcement Network (FinCEN), the following entities and individuals qualify as "U.S. Persons" for FBAR reporting purposes.

3.5.1.1: Citizens of the United States: This includes individuals born in the U.S., those who have acquired citizenship through naturalization, and children of U.S. citizens born abroad.

3.5.1.1: Residents of the United States: This typically refers to individuals who meet the substantial presence test or who hold a green card.

3.5.1.2: Domestic Entities: This encompasses corporations, partnerships, limited liability companies (LLCs), and other legal entities created or organized in the United States.

3.5.1.2: U.S. Persons for FBAR Purposes relate to Title 31.

Defining "U.S. Person" for Income Tax Purposes:

For income tax purposes under Title 26, the term 'U.S. Person' has a slightly different definition as it is articulated within the Internal Revenue Code (IRC). The following individuals and entities are categorised as 'U.S. Persons' for income tax obligations:

- **3.5.1.5:** Citizens of the United States: Similar to the FBAR definition, U.S. citizens are subject to income tax on their worldwide income, irrespective of their residence.
- **3.5.1.5:** Residents of the United States: This includes both lawful permanent residents (green card holders) and those who meet the substantial presence test, which is typically calculated based on the number of days an individual has been physically present in the U.S. over a three-year period.
- **3.5.1.7:** Domestic Corporations and Partnerships: Just like with FBAR, domestic entities created or organized in the U.S. are considered "U.S. Persons" for income tax purposes.
- **3.5.1.5:** U.S. persons for tax Purposes refers to Title 26.

U.S. persons are required to report their worldwide income to the Internal Revenue Service (IRS) and are eligible for various credits and deductions, such as the Foreign Tax Credit or the

Foreign Earned Income Exclusion, if applicable. Taxpayers are also required to file Form 1040, along with additional forms if they have foreign accounts or foreign entities, such as the FinCEN Form 114 for FBAR and Form 8938 for the Statement of Specified Foreign Financial Assets.

Key Differences Between FBAR and Income Tax Definitions

While the overarching concepts of "U.S. Person" in both FBAR and income tax contexts share similarities, the vital distinctions between them can significantly impact compliance.

- **3.6.1:** Threshold for Reporting: For FBAR, the reporting threshold is set at an aggregate value of $10,000 in foreign accounts, while for income tax, there is no minimum threshold for reporting worldwide income.
- **3.6.1:** Entities Covered: Both definitions cover individuals and entities; however, citizenship and residency nuances may lead to different compliance requirements. For instance, hybrid entities or foreign corporations owned by U.S. persons may be captured by one regulatory framework but not the other.
- **3.6.1:** Obligations: FBAR is concerned primarily with foreign bank accounts and financial assets, while income tax encompasses all forms of income, including wages, dividends, rents, and more.

Understanding the differences in "U.S. Person" definitions for FBAR and income tax purposes is critical for compliance and successful financial planning. Taxpayers should be vigilant in understanding their status, the associated reporting requirements, and the implications of their foreign activities. With the penalties for non-compliance being significant, having a clear demarcation between these definitions can help ensure that all necessary reporting obligations are met in a timely manner. As tax regulations and definitions may change, it is always prudent to consult with a tax professional knowledgeable about current laws and regulations to ensure full compliance.

"*Financial Account*"A financial account includes a:

- **3.7.1:** Bank account, such as a savings, demand, checking, deposit, time deposit, or any other account maintained with a financial institution or other person engaged in the business of a financial institution. A bank account set up to secure a credit card account is an example of a financial account. An insurance policy having a cash surrender value is an example of a financial account.
- **3.7.1:** Securities, securities derivatives, or other financial instruments account.
- **3.7.1:** Other financial accounts generally encompass any accounts in which the assets are held in a commingled fund and the account owner holds an equity interest in the fund.
- **3.7.1:** A mutual fund account is an example of such an account.
- **3.7.1:** Individual bonds, notes, or stock certificates held by the filer are not a financial account.

The location of an account, not the nationality of the financial institution with which the account is held, determines whether the account is in a foreign country. Any financial account (except accounts maintained with a U.S. military banking facility) located in a foreign country should be reported, even if the account is held with a branch of a United States financial institution located abroad. Generally, an account in a foreign country includes all geographical areas outside the United States.

"Having a Financial Interest In" a Foreign Financial Account

- **3.8.1:** A United States person has a financial interest in each account for which such person is the owner of record or has legal Title, whether the account is maintained for his benefit or the benefit of others, including non-United States persons.
- **3.8.1:** A United States person also has a financial interest in each bank, securities, or other financial account in a foreign country for which the owner of record or holder of legal Title is: a person acting as an agent, nominee, attorney, or in some other capacity on behalf of the U.S. person; or
- **3.8.1:** A corporation, whether foreign or domestic, in which a United States person owns directly or indirectly more than 50% of the total value of shares of stock; or
- **3.8.4:** A partnership, whether foreign or domestic, in which the United States person owns an interest in more than 50% of the profits (distributive share of income); or,
- **3.8.5:** A trust, whether foreign or domestic, in which the United States person either has a present beneficial interest in more than 50% of the assets or from which such person receives more than 50% of the current income.
- **3.8.6:** A bank is not required to file the FBAR to report a financial interest in an international interbank transfer.

"Signature Authority"

A person with a signature or other authority over a foreign financial account must file the FBAR even if the person has no financial interest in the account.

- **3.9.1:** A person has signature authority over an account if that person can control the disposition of money or other property in it by delivery of a document containing their signature (or their signature and that of one or more other persons) to the financial institution where the account is maintained.

Converting Foreign Currency to U.S. Dollars

3.10.1: Convert foreign currency by using the official exchange rate in effect at the end of the year in question for converting the foreign currency into USD. In valuing currency of a country that uses multiple exchange rates, use the rate that would apply if the currency in the account were converted into U.S. dollars at the close of the calendar year. The official Treasury Reporting Rates of Exchange for the previous quarter year can be obtained at "https://fiscaldata.treasury.gov/datasets/treasury-reporting-rates-exchange/treasury-reporting-rates-of-exchange."

Filing Date

- **3.11.1:** The FBAR must be filed on or before April 15 each calendar year
- **3.11.1:** The FBAR is considered filed when it is digitally filed and you receive an "Acknowledgement of Filing".
- **3.11.1:** You are allowed an Automatic Extension for October 15.
- **3.11.1:** You do not need to file for an extension

- **3.11.1:** Effective July 1, 2013, all FBAR reports must be filed electronically.

Chapter 4

Key Differences Between Form 8938 and FBAR

When it comes to disclosing foreign financial interests to the Internal Revenue Service (IRS) and other U.S. regulatory authorities, two forms are of central importance: Form 8938 and the Report of Foreign Bank and Financial Accounts (FBAR, officially known as FinCEN Form 114). While both forms serve to report foreign financial assets and accounts, they differ significantly in terms of requirements, thresholds, and the types of financial assets covered. This chapter will elucidate the key differences between Form 8938 and FBAR, providing clarity for taxpayers navigating foreign asset reporting.

Purpose of the Forms

- **Form 8938: Statement of Specified Foreign Financial Assets**

Form 8938 is part of the IRS regulations under the Foreign Account Tax Compliance Act (FATCA). Its primary objective is to report specified foreign financial assets owned by U.S. taxpayers. These assets could include foreign bank accounts, foreign stocks, mutual funds, and other foreign financial instruments. The information collected through Form 8938 helps the IRS track down tax evasion and ensure compliance with U.S. tax laws.

- **FBAR: Foreign Bank Account Report**

On the other hand, the FBAR is a requirement of the Bank Secrecy Act (BSA) and focuses specifically on foreign bank accounts. It is designed to combat money laundering and other illicit financial activities. FBAR requires U.S. taxpayers to report financial interests in or signature authority over foreign financial accounts when the total value exceeds a certain threshold.

Reporting Thresholds

- Form 8938 Thresholds: The reporting thresholds for Form 8938 depend on the taxpayer's filing status and whether they live in the U.S. or abroad:
- Unmarried taxpayers living in the U.S.** must file if the total value of specified foreign financial assets is over $50,000 on the last day of the tax year or over $75,000 at any time during the tax year.
- Married taxpayers living in the U.S **must file if the total value is over $100,000 on the last day of the year or over $150,000 at any time annually.
- Taxpayers living abroad: **The thresholds increase significantly, requiring a filing if the asset value exceeds $200,000 on the last day of the year or $300,000 at any point during the year for unmarried taxpayers, and double those amounts for married taxpayers.
- FBAR Thresholds: The FBAR has a more fundamental threshold: U.S. persons must file if their aggregate value of foreign financial accounts exceeds $10,000 at any time

during the calendar year. This lower threshold captures a wider array of foreign banking activities and is not dependent on the taxpayer's marital status or residency.

Types of Assets Reported Form

Form 8938: Asset Categories

Form 8938 covers a broad range of specified foreign financial assets, which can include but are not limited to foreign bank accounts.

- Foreign stocks or securities held in foreign accounts
- Interests in foreign entities
- Interests in certain foreign pension plans
- Foreign mutual funds

The form is detailed, requiring information about each asset, including value and whether the asset generates income. FBAR Asset Categories: FBAR is distinctly focused on the reporting of foreign financial accounts specifically:

- Bank accounts,
- Brokerage accounts,
- Mutual funds,
- Trust accounts, if they allow for deposits or withdrawals.

FBAR does not require details about the assets held within these accounts, making its reporting more streamlined than Form 8938.

Filing and Deadlines

Form 8938 Filing: Form 8938 is filed as part of the taxpayer's annual income tax return (**Form 1040**). The due date for Form 8938 aligns with the tax return deadline, typically April 15, with extensions available.

FBAR Filing: The FBAR must be filed separately from the income tax return and is due by April 15 as well, but it has an automatic extension to October 15. Taxpayers must file FBAR electronically through the Financial Crimes Enforcement Network's (FinCEN) BSA E-Filing System.

Penalties for Non-Compliance

Both forms carry significant penalties for non-compliance, but they differ in their structures:

Form 8938 Penalties

Failure to file Form 8938 can result in penalties starting at $10,000, with additional penalties of up to $50,000 for continued failure after IRS notification. If a taxpayer fully fails to report their assets, the penalties can be substantially higher.

FBAR Penalties

FBAR penalties are arguably more severe, with non-willful violations incurring a penalty of $10,000 for each violation. Willful violations are subject to much higher penalties, which can reach the greater of $100,000 or 50% of the account balance at the time of the violation.

Understanding the differences between Form 8938 and FBAR is crucial for U.S. taxpayers with foreign financial accounts and assets. While both forms aim to enhance transparency regarding foreign financial dealings, they serve different purposes, have different thresholds, cover varying types of financial interests, require separate filings, and invoke different consequences for non-compliance. Taxpayers should remain vigilant about their reporting obligations under both forms to avoid unnecessary penalties and ensure compliance with U.S. tax laws. As international finance becomes increasingly interconnected, staying

Information about these reporting requirements is more important than ever.

Chapter 5

Amendments and Corrections to FBAR

Introduction

The need for clarity, accuracy, and precision when submitting an FBAR cannot be overstated.

Inevitably, errors and omissions do occur. These can include failing to include a foreign financial account, failing to properly classify an account as single, joint, or signatory, using the wrong currency exchange rate when determining the value of a foreign financial account, and providing an incorrect account number or Financial Institution Address. This chapter will examine the necessity of filing a complete and accurate FBAR.

There are also instances where a taxpayer deliberately omits accounts with significant balances when submitting an FBAR. This is particularly problematic where the FBARS have been filed as part of an Offshore Disclosure. While it is difficult to know a taxpayer's intentions, the IRS views these tactics as willful concealment by the taxpayer.

Understanding Amendments and Corrections

Amendments refer to changes made to FinCEN Form 114. They can stem from using the currency exchange rate at the end of the year rather than the high watermark date, providing an incorrect account number, or the address of a financial institution related to a specific account. Errors can also include the failure to include all foreign financial accounts, failure to properly classify a foreign financial account as financial accounts "Owned Separately", "Owned Jointly," or "Where the filer has signature or other Authority", or using the wrong currency conversion rate. Perhaps most egregious is filing an FBAR that includes only accounts with low values but omits accounts with substantial balances.

The importance of amendments reflects upon the integrity of the taxpayer to properly disclose all relevant information, even if it results in the assessment of a civil FBAR Penalty. The method of amendment will depend upon the timing and the amount(s) in question, whether the Internal Revenue Service has commenced an examination, and the reason for the omission or error.

Reasons for Amending or Correcting an FBAR

Adding a Foreign Financial Account. This includes the foreign financial account that was excluded from the original FBAR filing.

Correcting the currency exchange rates used. It is common for taxpayers to incorrectly use the Treasury Average Currency Rate rather than the Treasury Year-End Currency Conversion, correcting the value. There are instances where a foreign financial institution fails to timely provide the taxpayer with the relevant information, resulting in the taxpayer using an estimated maximum account value or checking Box 15a, indicating that the "Maximum Account Value is Unknown". After much prodding, the foreign institution will provide the complete and correct information concerning a taxpayer's foreign financial accounts. It is noteworthy that since the enactment of the Foreign Assets Tax Compliance Act ("FATCA"), many foreign institutions will refuse to open an account for a U.S. Expat. In some cases, foreign institutions have, without notice to the taxpayer, closed an expat's accounts.

Failure to properly classify a Foreign Financial Account as owned 'Separately', 'Jointly', or an Account "Where the Filer has signatory or other authority, but not a financial interest in the account. Perhaps the most common error is where the taxpayer mistakenly indicates that he or she is only a "Signatory" on the account, only to learn that he or she is a 'joint' account holder.

Understanding the Maximum Account Value

If the understatement is nominal, amending the FBAR will suffice. However, in cases where the taxpayer substantially understates the maximum account value, or where the taxpayer adds an account with a substantial maximum value, simply amending the FBAR may be perceived as a "Quiet Disclosure", requiring the taxpayer to use one of the offshore disclosure protocols.

The process of correcting or amending is a previously filed FBAR. An FBAR can be amended as a stand-alone filing, or as part of a submission using the Voluntary Disclosure Practice rules or one of the two Streamlined Procedures. Determining which avenue the taxpayer elects, such a decision should not be made without the advice of an experienced and knowledgeable tax attorney.

VDP, Streamline Procedures or Simple Amendment

Before amending or correcting an FBAR, you must consider the nature and the scope of the amendment or correction as well as the amount of time that has passed since filing the original

FBAR. You must also be honest and ask the following questions.

- "Did I omit the accounts to avoid a penalty?"
- "Did I omit the accounts as a means of avoiding the use of the VDP and the significantly higher cost?"

If the error is ministerial, such as an incorrect account number or the wrong address for the foreign financial institution, and you are within the same year you filed, you should be able to amend the FBAR without any problem.

However, if you fail to report financial accounts with a substantial amount while only reporting accounts with small balances, you should consult with a lawyer to determine the method of informing the Internal Revenue Service. Quite clearly, the IRS will view this as a deliberate design to conceal your accounts.

If the FBARS were submitted as part of an Offshore Disclosure, you need to consult and retain an attorney to determine whether amendments should be made prior to or after disclosing the error or omission to the IRS. In particular, if you made a Streamlined submission to minimize or avoid paying any penalty.

Remember, you are certifying in the Statement of Facts that your failure to file complete and accurate FBARs was not the result of willful conduct.

Chapter 6

Using Quiet Disclosure to Cure FBAR Non-Compliance

The Consequences of Making a Quiet Disclosure

In the realm of international finance and taxation, few topics evoke as much concern and confusion as the failure to file FBARs. For U.S. citizens and residents with foreign financial interests, the FBAR is a crucial compliance requirement. The penalties for neglecting this obligation can be severe, often encouraging individuals to seek out options for resolution. One such option that has captured the attention of many is the concept of a "quiet disclosure". This chapter delves into the implications of failing to file FBARs, the allure of quiet disclosures, and the risks associated with this approach.

Understanding FBAR Requirements

The FBAR, officially known as FinCEN Form 114, is designed to combat offshore tax evasion and ensure transparency in foreign financial holdings. The U.S. Department of the Treasury mandates that any U.S. person with a financial interest in or signature authority over foreign financial accounts exceeding $10,000 at any time during the calendar year must file this report. The broad definition of "U.S. person", encompassing citizens, residents, and entities, means that many individuals may unwittingly find themselves violating these regulations.

Consequences of Non-Compliance

The penalties for failing to file FBARs can vary significantly depending on whether the violation is deemed willful or non-willful. Non-willful violations can incur penalties of up to $10,000 per FBAR Report per year, while willful violations can lead to penalties of the greater of $100,000 or 50% of the account balance at the time of the violation. Such penalties can be financially devastating and have long-lasting implications for your personal and professional reputation.

Given these consequences, many individuals may feel cornered when they realize they have failed to comply with FBAR requirements. This sense of urgency often pushes them toward exploring options for remediation that may appear less daunting or burdensome.

After learning of the FBAR filing requirements, some taxpayers will simply bypass making an offshore disclosure and start filing FBARs. This maneuver is seen by the IRS as an act of concealment and deception, usually resulting in the very least the assessment of the willful FBAR penalty and the potential application of civil tax penalties, most notably the 75% Civil Tax Penalty.

The Allure of Quiet Disclosures

A "Quiet Disclosure" typically refers to filing past-due FBARs and amending tax returns for unreported foreign income without notifying the IRS of the delinquency. Individuals may opt for this route, hoping to avoid scrutiny and penalties by presenting their filings in the context of an Offshore Disclosure.

The siren call of quiet disclosures is often founded on a few key beliefs:

- **Avoiding Detection:** Many believe that by simply filing the overdue forms, they can escape significant consequences or investigations by the IRS. The thought process is that if the filing is done quietly, it minimizes the likelihood of the IRS becoming aware of the past non-compliance.
- **Cost vs. Penalties:** For some, the potential penalties for non-compliance appear to outweigh the risks associated with coming forward voluntarily through an offshore disclosure. This leads individuals to weigh the immediate costs of penalties and legal fees against the perceived benefits of keeping their financial issues hidden.
- **Desire for Closure**: Living in fear of potential repercussions can be mentally and emotionally taxing. For many who want to put the issue behind them, the idea of filing the necessary forms and moving on provides a significant appeal.

The Risks of Making a Quiet Disclosure

Despite the attractive nature of quiet disclosures, this approach is fraught with significant risks. Emerging from the shadows of past non-compliance often proves to be more complex and precarious than individuals initially anticipate.

This could reveal even more serious issues. Keep in mind

that if you failed to file a timely FBAR, you must select one of the reasons in the drop-down menu on FinCEN Form.

- **Increased IRS Scrutiny:** The IRS has implemented various measures to identify quietly disclosed returns, particularly after the launch of high-profile initiatives targeting offshore accounts. Filing overdue FBARs under the radar raises the risk of triggering an audit and further Investigation 114.
- **Willful Penalties**: If the IRS determines that a taxpayer was willfully non-compliant, the penalties could escalate dramatically. An individual may believe they can avoid penalties through a quiet disclosure, only to face the harsh consequences of willful neglect.
- **Long-Term Consequences:** Even if an individual successfully files a quiet disclosure, the repercussions may linger. Those who choose not to disclose their non-compliance through official channels might later encounter difficulties securing loans, financing, or even pursuing international opportunities due to the taint of potential criminal liability.

While the lure of a quiet disclosure may seem appealing to those grappling with the pressure of unfiled FBARs, the associated risks can outweigh the temporary relief it offers. Navigating the complexities of foreign financial compliance requires careful consideration, particularly in choosing a course of action that minimizes potential exposure to severe penalties and legal ramifications.

Ultimately, the decision to make a quiet disclosure should be made with a solid understanding of one's financial situation, a clear assessment of the risks involved, and ideally, guidance from a qualified tax professional. While the lure of a quiet resolution may be tempting, the repercussions of that choice are substantial and far-reaching, underscoring the importance of compliance and transparency in managing foreign financial interests.

Chapter 7

Concealing Foreign Accounts: The Role of Shell Companies, Nominees, and Advisors

Using a Shell Company, Nominee, or Third Party to Avoid Filing FBAR

The Report of Foreign Bank and Financial Accounts (FBAR) is a crucial instrument established by the United States government to combat tax evasion and promote transparency concerning foreign financial accounts. U.S. persons with an aggregate value exceeding $10,000 in foreign accounts are required to disclose this information annually. While compliance is essential, some individuals attempt to evade these regulations using various methods, including shell companies, nominees, or third parties. This chapter explores these ill-conceived strategies, elucidates the legal implications, and underscores the importance of compliance with FBAR filing requirements.

Understanding FBAR Requirements

Before delving into evasion tactics, it is important to grasp the underlying purpose of FBAR regulations. Instituted under the Bank Secrecy Act (BSA), the FBAR requires U.S. citizens, residents, and certain entities to report foreign financial accounts if they have signature authority or financial interest in those accounts. Failure to file can lead to severe penalties, both civil and criminal.

The Allure of Avoidance Tactics

Some individuals seek to circumvent these stringent regulations by employing creative strategies. The use of shell companies,, nominees, and third parties has gained traction among those wishing to shield their foreign assets from scrutiny.

The offshore tax evasion playbook, which has been around for quite some time with some slight variations, is still in use. Some of the practices include, but are not limited to, forming an offshore nominee entity in a blacklisted or designated tax haven jurisdiction and opening Foreign Financial Accounts ("FFA") in the name of the nominee, shell company or other entity to obscure the identity of the true account owner. In many cases, the true account owner will secretly retain beneficial ownership in the FFA or asset as a means of retaining control and dominion over the account proceeds.

A savvy tax cheat will, on occasion, have the mail related to the offshore account or asset held at the foreign financial institution. Then, the true account owner will periodically travel to the foreign country to retrieve the mail in person or make arrangements for someone else to. Alternatively, the account owner will meet with a representative from the foreign financial institution in the U.S. for the handoff.

For their part, Foreign Financial Institutions ("FFIs"), wealth management firms, and other foreign counterparts have historically accommodated, promoted, and actively facilitated the secreting of offshore assets and income by U.S. taxpayers in exchange for receiving substantial bank, legal, and advisory fees. Foreign governments have also been complicit by either turning a blind eye to these illicit practices or by relying on bank secrecy laws. That has all changed thanks to U.S. global enforcement initiatives, international cooperation, and the recent 80 billion dollars received by the IRS.

The Path to Compliance

Rather than resorting to dubious strategies, individuals with foreign accounts should focus on compliance. This involves:

Understanding Reporting Requirements:

- Familiarizing oneself with FBAR requirements, including who must file and the types of accounts that need to be reported.
- Accurate Record Keeping: Maintaining detailed records regarding foreign accounts, including account numbers, financial institutions, and balances.

Seeking Professional Guidance: Consulting tax professionals or attorneys experienced in international taxation can help individuals navigate compliance and mitigate risks.

While the allure of using shell companies, nominees, or third parties to avoid filing an FBAR may be tempting, the legal ramifications make such paths perilous. Non-compliance not only jeopardizes financial stability through potential penalties but also tarnishes personal integrity. Ultimately, embracing transparency and adhering to regulatory requirements is not only prudent but necessary for maintaining financial health and legal compliance in an increasingly interconnected world.

Chapter 8

Understanding The Non-Willful and Willful Civil FBAR Penalties and the Reasonable Cause Defense

The Report of Foreign Bank and Financial Accounts (FBAR), formally known as FinCEN Form 114, must be filed by U.S. persons with foreign financial accounts exceeding $10,000 in aggregate value at any time during the calendar year. The penalties for failing to comply can be severe, particularly in distinguishing between willful and non-willful violations. This chapter explores the complexities surrounding the imposition of civil penalties for FBAR violations, addressing the burden of proof required by the government and the implications of a reasonable cause defence.

Understanding FBAR Penalties

FBAR violations attract two primary types of civil penalties, which differ significantly based on the taxpayer's actions: willful and non-willful violations. The distinction is crucial because it not only affects the severity of penalties but also the legal defences available to taxpayers.

Non-Wilful Penalties

Non-willful violations occur when a taxpayer fails to file the FBAR due to negligence, inadvertence, or a misunderstanding of the law, rather than due to any intention to conceal assets. Under the Bank Secrecy Act, non-willful violations can incur a penalty of up to $10,000 per violation. Importantly, if the taxpayer can provide reasonable cause for their failure to report, this may mitigate the penalty or even lead to a waiver.

Burden of Proof. In cases of non-willful violations, the burden of proof lies with the taxpayer to demonstrate reasonable cause for their non-compliance. The standard for reasonable cause is often evaluated on a case-by-case basis, considering factors such as the taxpayer's financial sophistication, efforts made to comply, and reliance on professional advisors.

Willful Penalties

In stark contrast, willful violations arise when a taxpayer knowingly disregards the law's requirements or acts with reckless disregard of the facts that would require FBAR filing. Willful violations can lead to penalties equating to the greater of $100,000 or 50% of the balance in the foreign accounts at the time of the violation.

Burden of Proof for Willful Penalties. The burden of proof shifts to the IRS, which must establish willfulness by making a showing by a preponderance of evidence. This lower level of proof needed provides the IRS with a relatively easy avenue for asserting the willful FBAR penalty. Failure to file FBAR despite being advised by a tax professional of the need to file FBARs as well as failure to make the Schedule B disclosures, is sufficient to sustain a willful FBAR Penalty.

The Reasonable Cause Defense

The reasonable cause defence is a critical aspect in defending against non-willful FBAR penalties. This defence hinges on the taxpayer's ability to present persuasive evidence that, despite failing to file their FBAR, they had a legitimate reason for doing so.

Establishing Reasonable Cause to successfully argue reasonable cause, a taxpayer might include:

- **Evidence of Efforts to Comply:** Demonstrating initiatives undertaken to understand and fulfill their reporting responsibilities, such as consulting tax professionals or reaching out to the IRS to seek clarification.
- **Circumstantial Factors:** Presenting documentation reflecting extenuating circumstances that may have prevented compliance, including serious medical issues, natural disasters, or significant life events.
- **Financial Hardship:** If applicable, illustrating that the taxpayer lacked the means to comply due to financial hardship or other mitigating factors.

Challenges with the Defense

While the reasonable cause defence may serve as an effective shield against non-willful penalties, it is not without challenges. The IRS has broad discretion in determining what constitutes reasonable cause, and taxpayers may face difficulties in effectively presenting their case. Therefore, proper documentation and expert legal guidance are essential in establishing this defence.

Navigating the complexities of FBAR penalties requires an understanding of the distinct boundaries between wilful and non-wilful violations. The stakes are high. While non-willful violations allow for a defense of reasonable cause, willful violations expose taxpayers to far more severe repercussions. With the burden of proof often shifting between the IRS and the taxpayer, the necessity of sound legal advice and thorough record-keeping cannot be overstated. Ultimately, awareness and proactive measures can mitigate the risks associated with FBAR compliance and protect against substantial penalties. Is the Reasonable Cause Defense Available in Wilful Civil FBAR Cases?

Non-Willful vs. Willful Violations

The distinction between non-willful and willful violations is critical. Non-willful violations typically incur a penalty of $10,000 per violation, while willful violations can lead to penalties of the greater of $100,000 or 50% of the account balance at the time of the violation. The IRS and the courts take willful violations seriously, interpreting them as acts of intentional disregard for the law.

The Reasonable Cause Defense

The reasonable cause defense is a legal principle that allows taxpayers to avoid penalties if they can demonstrate that they had a reasonable basis for failing to comply with tax laws. In certain tax contexts, establishing reasonable cause can absolve a taxpayer of liability, resting on the premise that the individual acted with honesty and good faith.

Application to FBAR Penalties

In the context of FBAR penalties, the Internal Revenue Service (IRS) has indicated that reasonable cause may be considered as a defence in non-willful cases. The IRS's 2014 FBAR Penalty Guidelines suggest that if a taxpayer can show they had reasonable cause for their failure to report, they may not be subject to penalties.

Exploration of Willful Civil FBAR CasesIn willful civil FBAR cases, the stakes are raised significantly. The courts and the IRS have maintained a firm stance that willfulness indicates a conscious choice to disregard the reporting requirements. Because of this, the applicability of the reasonable cause defence in such cases merits deeper examination.

Statutory Interpretation and Judicial Precedents

A pivotal element to understanding the unavailability of a reasonable cause defense in willful cases lies in the statutory language of the BSA and pertinent judicial interpretations. The statute does not provide for a reasonable cause defence in the context of willful violations, and the courts have consistently reinforced the notion that willful conduct implies that there can be no reasonable cause.

Judicial precedent shows that the assumption of ignorance or misunderstanding of the law will not relieve individuals from penalties incurred through willful misconduct. The case of U.S. v. Williams emphasizes this distinction, wherein the court ruled that wilfulness, as defined in the context of FBAR violations, precludes the application of reasonable cause as a defence against penalties.

Consequences for Taxpayers

The inability to invoke a reasonable cause defence in willful FBAR cases places considerable pressure on taxpayers. Individuals facing allegations of willful violations may find themselves exposed to substantial penalties, regardless of their subjective belief about their compliance. This lack of a reasonable cause defence can lead to a chilling effect, dissuading taxpayers from coming forward and rectifying their reporting failures or seeking advice.

The reasonable cause defence, while available in non-willful FBAR cases, is decidedly absent in wilful civil FBAR cases. The stringent interpretations by the courts and the IRS underscore the seriousness with which willful conduct is treated under FBAR regulations. This distinct lack of a defense emphasizes the necessity for U.S. taxpayers to engage in proactive compliance, educating themselves on reporting obligations and seeking professional guidance where needed to avoid the severe consequences associated with willful violations. As the landscape of international finance continues to evolve, understanding these nuances will be paramount for individuals and entities navigating the complexities of foreign financial compliance.

Chapter 9

IRS Criminal Investigations and Global Enforcement Initiatives

The Challenge, International non-compliance, has become a significant area of concern and focus for the Internal Revenue Service. Based upon recent criminal prosecutions and convictions by the Department of Justice and global tax enforcement initiatives, it is clear that international tax is a top priority for the IRS and that the agency will vigorously pursue offshore tax evasion, no matter how remote or secret the location. The increased scrutiny is based upon a number of factors.

IRS Criminal Investigation

As the global economy continues to grow, the tax implications of conducting business outside of the United States and attempts at circumventing tax and financial reporting have not gone unnoticed by the IRS Criminal Investigation (CI) Certain U.S. taxpayers have engaged and continue to engage in international tax avoidance schemes and cross-border financial transactions, designed to avoid detection by the IRS.

In response to this challenge, the IRS has developed a Service-wide Approach to International Tax Administration to improve voluntary compliance with the international tax provisions, financial reporting requirements, and information return obligations.

Criminal investigation plays a significant role in the coordination of international tax compliance efforts and ferreting out individuals and business entities attempting to avoid detection. They work closely with international law enforcement partners as well as federal, state, and local law enforcement agencies to investigate financial fraud.

This elite division of the IRS has approximately 3,500 employees worldwide, 2,500 of whom are special agents who investigate violations of the Internal Revenue Code and related violations of U.S. financial reporting statutes. According to statistical data on the IRS website, Criminal Investigation's conviction rate is one of the highest in federal law enforcement, with a very small number of prosecutions ever going to trial.

This impressive conviction rate is attributable to several initiatives aimed at discovering U.S. taxpayers with undeclared foreign financial accounts, as well as indicators of offshore tax evasion. The initiatives include the following.

Whistleblowers and Informants

The IRS Whistleblower Office pays money to people who blow the whistle on persons who fail to pay the tax that they owe or attempt to conceal their foreign assets. The IRS uses information provided by the whistleblower, and it can award the whistleblower up to 30% of the additional tax, penalty, and other amounts it collects.

As an example, in Sept. 2012, the IRS announced that Bradley Birkenfeld, a former banker at UBS, would receive a $104 million whistle-blower award for revealing the secrets of the Swiss banking system. By divulging the schemes that UBS used to aid American citizens in dodging their taxes, Mr. Birkenfeld led to an investigation that greatly diminished Switzerland's status as a secret haven for American tax evaders and allowed the Treasury to recover billions in unpaid taxes.

The Civil Summons Process (John Doe Summons)

A John Doe Summons is an IRS summons authorised by Internal Revenue Code Section 7609(f). Unlike other IRS summonses, it does not list the name of the taxpayer under investigation because the taxpayer is unknown to the IRS. With a normal summons, the IRS seeks information about a specific taxpayer whose identity it knows. In contrast, a John Doe summons allows the IRS to obtain the names of all taxpayers in a certain group. Because of this, a John Doe summons is ideal for pursuing tax shelter investors or account holders at a financial institution.

Requests under a Tax Treaty or Mutual Information Exchange agreement.

The United States has tax treaties and tax information exchange agreements (TIEAs) with many countries that provide for the exchange of information on tax matters. Tax treaties or mutual information exchange agreements are bilateral agreements that establish a legal basis for the exchange of tax information relating to persons and entities between the signatories. These agreements are the result of an initiative by the Organization for Economic

Cooperation and Development (OECD) to improve the transparency of financial flows between countries.

Voluntary Disclosures of U.S. Taxpayers Seeking to Avoid Criminal Prosecution

In November of 2018, the Department of Justice announced the new Voluntary Disclosure Practice Rules (VDPR), replacing the Offshore Voluntary Disclosure Program (OVDP). Which was terminated on September 18, 2018. This program puts U.S. expat account holders at immediate risk because it requires that foreign financial institutions disclose to the IRS the names and account details of all current and former account holders of expats living abroad or who have offshore accounts. The VDPR is discussed in depth in Chapter 11.

If the IRS can show that a U.S. taxpayer had knowledge of the FBAR regulations and failed to comply, the person may be subject to civil and criminal penalties, including heavy fines and possible jail time. Often, these disclosures result in the taxpayer "ratting out" other individuals, such as accountants, lawyers and facilitators, as a way to mitigate their circumstances.

FATCA and Related Legislative and Regulatory Development. The Foreign Account Tax Compliance Act (FATCA) is one of the efforts the U.S. government has put in place to combat offshore tax evasion. FATCA, enacted in 2010, aims to target non-payment of federal taxes by U.S. taxpayers through the use of foreign accounts. FATCA requires foreign institutions and global banks to identify any U.S. clients with more than $50,000 USD in their accounts. The Act requires foreign financial institutions to come clean to the IRS about their U.S.-owned accounts or face, in some cases, a 30% withholding tax on certain U.S.-source payments that are made to them.

Tax cheats will find it increasingly difficult to find favorable havens for overseas tax evasion. With tough legislation, global partnering, and CI's financial investigative skills, the days of overseas tax evasion and financial crimes are numbered.

OECD Common Reporting Standards

Today, the necessity for robust frameworks to enhance tax transparency and combat tax evasion has never been more crucial. The Organization for Economic Co-operation and Development (OECD) has been at the forefront of this effort, leading initiatives that promote effective tax governance and collaboration among nations.

One of the cornerstone achievements in this journey is the establishment of the Common Reporting Standards (CRS). The following discussion examines the origins, components, implementation, and implications of the OECD Common Reporting Standards, illuminating its importance in fostering international tax compliance.

The Common Reporting Standards encompass several core components that together create a comprehensive framework for the automatic exchange of information. The components include standardized reporting, the development of due diligence procedures and a reporting framework, and data security and confidentiality.

Though the CRS has significant advances, it has not been without its detractors, who have opposed the implementation of the CRS. In particular, developing countries maintain that the CRS is beneficial only to large developed countries and undermines the economic growth of developing countries. Recently, a coalition of African countries has called for the OECD to be disbanded and its functions assumed by the United Nations.

As of the 2023 reporting period, over 100 jurisdictions are committed to the CRS, with many already participating in the automatic exchange of information, representing a significant global shift towards tax transparency and cooperation. It is important to note that the United States is not a signatory to the CRS, in part, due to FATCA.

Chapter: Financial Action Task Force (FATF)

The Financial Action Task Force (FATF) is an intergovernmental organization founded in 1989 to combat money laundering, terrorist financing, and other threats to the integrity of the international financial system. Established initially to develop policies to combat money laundering, the FATF has evolved to address a broader range of financial crimes, including the financing of weapons of mass destruction. This section examines the history, structure, functions, and impact of the FATF, as well as the challenges it faces in a constantly changing global landscape.

The FATF was established in the late 1980s in response to growing concerns over the rise of money laundering, particularly in the wake of the drug trade and the increasing sophistication of financial criminals. The G7 nations spearheaded the initiative at a summit in Paris, leading to the creation of the FATF as a policy-making body. The organization's initial task was to propose measures and policies that member countries could adopt to counter money laundering.

Over time, as terrorism financing became a central concern following significant global incidents like the September 11 attacks, the FATF broadened its mandate to include the prevention of terrorist financing. Its guidelines and recommendations became more comprehensive, encompassing a wider spectrum of financial crimes and the ways these crimes could disrupt national and international security.

The primary functions of the FATF are to: develop standards, evaluate and monitor compliance, promote international cooperation, and issue guidance. Since the FATF's work has led to greater transparency in financial systems worldwide, enhancing the capability of governments and institutions to detect and deter illicit activities. Countries that adhere to FATF standards have improved their regulatory frameworks, increased inter-agency collaboration, and bolstered the capacity of law enforcement to investigate and prosecute financial crimes.

The U.S. Government is also working with other governments and law enforcement agencies to share knowledge and support the development of expertise in financial investigation techniques and forensic accounting procedures through its developed and accredited training course, Financial Investigative Training (FIT).

Joint Chiefs of Global Tax Enforcement

The roots of the JCGTE can be traced back to the global financial crisis of 2008, which exposed significant weaknesses in tax systems worldwide. Faced with dwindling revenues and rising deficits, governments were compelled to rethink their approaches to tax enforcement. The Pandora Papers and Offshore Leaks continually revealed the extent of tax evasion strategies employed by individuals and corporations, sparking public outcry and calls for reform. In 2015, the G20, in tandem with the Organisation for Economic Co-operation and Development (OECD), proposed a transformative framework for global tax reform, establishing the foundations upon which the JCGTE would be built.

The JCGTE was created in response to the urgent need for enhanced international cooperation in tackling tax evasion. By uniting tax authorities from various nations, the initiative aimed to foster information sharing, standardize tax regulations, and create a unified front against transnational tax crimes.

The JCGTE is a cooperative consortium that includes tax enforcement agencies from member countries, representatives from international financial institutions, and experts in financial law. The governing body is composed of representatives from each participating country, ensuring that both developed and developing nations have a voice in how global tax enforcement should evolve.

The Joint Chiefs of Global Tax Enforcement focuses on information sharing, standardization of practices in tax enforcement, training and capacity building, and joint investigations.

The Joint Chiefs of Global Tax Enforcement is a pioneering

initiative reflecting the necessity of cooperation in the fight against tax evasion. As global economic landscapes continue to evolve, the JCGTE will play a critical role in ensuring that tax systems are not only robust but also butal. By fostering collaboration, sharing information, and standardizing practices, the JCGTE sets the stage for a more equitable global financial system where tax compliance is the norm rather than the exception.

Financial Action Task Force: Interpol Red Notice

In a world where crime knows no borders, international cooperation is vital for enforcing justice. Among the tools at the disposal of law enforcement agencies worldwide, the Interpol Red Notice stands out as a significant mechanism for tracking and apprehending fugitives who have evaded justice. We will explore the origins, purposes, processes, and implications of Red Notices.

Interpol, or the International Criminal Police Organization, was established in 1923 to facilitate international police cooperation. With 195 countries as members, it serves as a vital link between national law enforcement agencies, enabling them to work together in the pursuit of criminals. One of the primary functions of Interpol is issuing notices, alerts that communicate information about crimes, investigations, and fugitives across borders.

A Red Notice (the Notice) is a request to law enforcement worldwide to locate and provisionally arrest a person pending extradition, surrender, or similar legal action. It is based on an arrest warrant or court order issued by the judicial authorities in their quest. Member countries apply their laws in deciding whether to arrest a person. “https://www.interpol.int/en.”

The notice contains essential information about the individual, including their identity, the alleged offence, the legal basis for the request, and any relevant details that could aid in the apprehension process. Interpol's commitment to neutrality and respect for human rights ensures that the notices adhere to strict guidelines, barring their use for political, military, racial, or religious reasons.

The primary purpose of a notice is to alert law enforcement agencies around the world to the presence of individuals who are wanted for prosecution or to serve a sentence. It serves to enhance international cooperation in the fight against transnational crime, allowing countries to share information effectively and work collaboratively.

The Process for Issuing a Red Notice Involves Several Steps.

- **Request Submission:** A member country submits a request to Interpol through its National Central Bureau (NCB), accompanied by the relevant judicial documents.
- **Evaluation:** Interpol's General Secretariat evaluates its quest to ensure it meets the organization's criteria, including an assessment of the legal basis and assurance that it is not politically motivated.
- **Issuance:** If approved, the Red Notice is disseminated to all Interpol member countries, which can use it to identify and apprehend the individual.

- **Further Actions:** Upon locating the fugitive, the country's law enforcement may arrest the individual based on their national laws, typically leading to extradition proceedings if applicable.

The Role of Internal Revenue Attachés in Global Taxation

Criminal Investigation has expanded its overseas presence by assigning attachés to key foreign embassies and consulates. In an era of globalization, the complexities of taxation have expanded beyond national borders. Traditional tax frameworks, once limited to domestic activities, now necessitate an international perspective to address the growing challenges posed by cross-border transactions, transfer pricing, and tax compliance. Within this framework, Attachés play a pivotal role in shaping international tax policy and promoting cooperation among countries.

Internal Revenue Service Attachés are officials stationed in embassies or consulates who specialize in tax issues. One of the primary functions of the Internal Revenue Attaché is to provide expert advice to their home country's government on international tax issues. They assess the tax implications of various international agreements, provide insights into global taxation trends, and recommend strategic actions in negotiations with other jurisdictions. By keeping their governments informed about the latest developments in international taxation, they ensure that their countries are well-equipped to navigate the evolving landscape.

Attachés also play an instrumental role in the negotiation and implementation of bilateral tax treaties aimed at preventing double taxation and facilitating cross-border trade and investment.

Moreover, Attachés are instrumental in their solution of disputes that arise from differing interpretations of tax laws. Finally, Attachés facilitate the navigation of Digital Taxation.

Chapter 10

Offshore Disclosure Options: Curing Tax Compliance and Foreign Financial Reporting Issues

Introduction: Coming Into Compliance – Selecting an Offshore Disclosure Option. For many, managing U.S. tax and financial reporting obligations responsibly can seem insurmountable, in particular, taxpayers who traditionally self-prepare their returns may not be familiar with the FBAR reporting requirements, nor have ever had occasion to run across the topic online. Some taxpayers deceitfully try to conceal their ownership in foreign financial accounts by either placing the accounts in a foreign shell company that the taxpayer retains beneficial ownership in or by arranging with a foreign financial advisor to have the taxpayer's entire foreign bank statements sent to their foreign address, rather than the taxpayer's U.S. address.

Each year, the latter group will visit their CPA, enrolled agent, or tax preparer. The tax preparer will typically ask the client to complete a tax organizer. Most tax organisers will contain questions related to the existence of foreign financial accounts as well as a foreign source income.

In completing the tax organizer, these individuals will respond 'No' to the question concerning the existence of foreign financial accounts. They will also answer 'No' when asked if they received any foreign source income. The CPA will then prepare the tax returns and either answer 'no' to question 7a, Part III of

Schedule B, or not include Schedule B as part of the tax return. In addition, the tax preparer would not file an FBAR or Form 8938, if applicable, based upon the client's answers contained in the tax organizer.

Both groups need the assistance of a knowledgeable and experienced tax attorney in selecting an offshore disclosure protocol that will result in the least amount of financial pain and bring the matter to final disposition. In this context, the process of "coming into compliance" becomes essential for those who have previously not fully disclosed their offshore accounts or income. Understanding the various offshore disclosure options available is a critical first step toward rectifying past oversights and aligning with legal requirements.

Finally, some taxpayers use the Streamlined Procedures simply due to the cost of representation and the applicable penalties associated with using the Voluntary Disclosure Practice Rule. In many cases, Groups 2 and 3 are present.

We will discuss the offshore disclosure options that are available, ranging from the Voluntary Disclosure Practice Rules to using the Streamlined Procedures. We will highlight the importance of selecting the right option based on an individual's circumstances, including the nature of undisclosed assets, potential penalties, and the desire for legal resolution and criminal risk. Finally, we will look at recent developments in the first prosecution ever of a taxpayer who submitted a false Statement of Facts. As tax compliance evolves, so too do the strategies for effectively addressing past discrepancies and fostering a transparent financial future.

By examining the various avenues available for coming into compliance, the discussion that follows aims to empower individuals and entities with the knowledge necessary to make informed decisions, ensuring adherence to regulatory mandates while safeguarding one's financial integrity.

The Available Offshore Disclosure Options

Today, we live in the Global Society, and as a result, financial transactions often extend beyond domestic borders, leading individuals and corporations to explore global wealth management strategies. One critical aspect of this landscape is understanding offshore disclosure options. These avenues permit taxpayers to report foreign financial accounts, investments, and income while complying with local and international tax laws. This chapter delves into the available offshore disclosure options, providing clarity on their mechanisms, advantages, risks, and underlying regulations.

Understanding Offshore Disclosure

Offshore disclosure refers to the legal obligation of individuals and entities to report certain foreign financial interests and income to their home country's tax authority. These disclosures are vital to ensuring transparency in international finance and combating tax evasion. In recent years, governments worldwide have ramped up efforts to track unreported offshore accounts, leading to severe penalties for non-compliance. Thus, understanding available disclosure options becomes crucial for taxpayers with assets overseas.

The Offshore Voluntary Disclosure Practice Rules

In an increasingly globalized economy, many taxpayers find themselves with offshore assets or income that requires careful consideration regarding compliance with tax laws and financial reporting obligations. The Voluntary Disclosure Practice (VDP) offers a pathway for taxpayers to rectify past non-compliance related to offshore matters while potentially minimizing penalties. However, taxpayers must also consider the downside risk of prosecution when using the Voluntary Disclosure Practice Rules. With the amendment to Form 14457, the taxpayer, a condition of eligibility, now must admit that his or her failure to file FBARs and to report Foreign Income was 'Willful'. In addition, the admissions the taxpayer must now make as a condition of participating in the program will more than likely foreclose any possibility of negotiating the Willful Civil FBAR Penalty.

Understanding the Voluntary Disclosure Practice Rules

Before embarking on the offshore disclosure journey, taxpayers must understand the purpose and implications of the Voluntary Disclosure Practice. The VDPR is designed to encourage taxpayers to come forward to disclose undisclosed income, assets, or transactions before they are discovered by tax authorities. By voluntarily disclosing this information, taxpayers may benefit from avoiding time in prison and the prospect of being left with some of their wealth.

Step-by-Step Process for Offshore Disclosure

The following steps outline the process a taxpayer should follow to make an effective offshore disclosure under the Voluntary Disclosure Practice.

Step 1: Seek Professional Guidance. It is wise for taxpayers to seek professional guidance from tax advisors or legal experts who specialize in offshore tax matters. Their expertise can help navigate complexities, ensure compliance with legal requirements, and optimize outcomes.

Step 2: Under the VDPR eligibility, eligibilyt for making an offshore disclosure using the VDPR. Here is a two-part electronic application (Form 14457) process to request participation in the VDP. Part I is a preclearance request, and Part II is a determination of your preliminary acceptance.

Once CI receives your Part I and has determined that you are eligible, they will send you or your counsel, if you are represented, a "pre-clearance letter". It is important to note that preclearance only determines your eligibility for the practice but does not guarantee preliminary acceptance into the practice.

Step 3: If you are pre-cleared, you have 45 days in which to electronically submit Part II of Form 14457. Criminal Investigation will review your Part II submissions, and if approved, will issue a 'Preliminary Acceptance Letter'.

If you are approved, CI will send Form 14457 to the Civil Division, and the case will be assigned to a Civil Examiner. The Civil Examiner will contact you and, in all likelihood, request that you provide relevant documents. As part of the process, you will be required to provide a statement acknowledging your willful failure to comply with tax or tax-related obligations.

If you are unable to submit Part II of the application within 45 days of the Pre-Clearance letter, you may request to withdraw from the VDP. You may also seek a one-time 45-day extension.

A voluntary disclosure will not be considered timely if the IRS has not received all the required submissions within 45 days and the IRS has commenced a civil examination or criminal investigation.

Received information from a third party (e.g., informant, other governmental agency, John Doe summons, etc.) alerting us to your noncompliance.

Acquired information directly related to your specific noncompliance from a criminal enforcement action (e.g., search warrant, grand jury subpoena, etc.). An integral part of the disclosure process is the collection and organization of all relevant documentation. This may include:

- Bank statements and financial records from offshore accounts.
- Records of transactions involving offshore income or assets.
- Any correspondence with foreign institutions.
- Tax returns and filing history related to the offshore assets or income.

Step 4: Prepare Amended Returns and FBARs.

The "Disclosure Period" for filing amended tax returns is 6

and 8 years for FBARs. You will be required to file 6 years of amended income tax returns and 8 years of FBARs, or if applicable, amended FBARs. You must calculate the civil tax penalties as well as the FBAR penalties.

Step 5: Prepare the Voluntary Disclosure Submission

The next step is to prepare a formal disclosure submission, typically including:

- A detailed letter outlining the nature of the offshore income/assets and the reason for non-compliance.
- Completed tax returns for the years in question, reflecting the accurate amounts.
- A breakdown of the taxpayer's total liability, including tax owed, penalties, and interest.
- Copies of original tax returns for the disclosure period.
- Copies of original or amended FBAR's together with the acknowledgements of filing, calculate the 75% Civil Fraud Penalty on any additional income tax due. This is in lieu of the 20% accuracy penalty and the 25% delinquency penalty. Calculate the Offshore Penalty.

Step 6: Submit the Disclosure

Once the disclosure package is complete, taxpayers should submit it to the IRS Office in Austin, Texas. You may also be able to submit some of the documents electronically, if permitted, to ensure expedited processing.

Step 7: Address Payment of Outstanding Liabilities

When making the submission, the taxpayer should include payment. Generally, one check to cover the Title 26 tax, penalties, and interest, as well as the Title 31 FBAR Penalty.

If the taxpayer does not have the resources to pay the tax, penalties, interest, and FBAR penalty, he or she should still submit the disclosure package. However, keep in mind that the internet is accruing.

Navigating the process of making an offshore disclosure using the Voluntary Disclosure Practice Rules is a critical step for taxpayers seeking to rectify past non-compliance by following these structured steps. However, such a decision should not be made without consultation with an experienced and knowledgeable tax attorney.

Sometimes, taxpayers who have criminal risk will try to use the Streamlined Procedures, since there is either no penalty on Streamlined Foreign Disclosures or a 5% Penalty on Streamlined Domestic Disclosures. You also escape the 75% Civil Fraud Penalty. See what happened to one taxpayer below.

Streamlined Offshore Procedures and the Streamlined Domestic Offshore Procedures

For taxpayers with minimal criminal risk, the Streamlined Filing Compliance Procedures provide the taxpayer can establish that the conduct was not "Willful" (SFCP). This protocol allows qualifying individuals to come into compliance by filing delinquent tax returns and FBAR reports. The current Streamlined Procedures came about when the IRS finally acknowledged that "One Size

Does Not Fit All". The Streamlined benefits include the following.

Reduced Penalties: Non-willful offenders may face fewer consequences than those who willfully fail to disclose their offshore accounts. Depending on the circumstances, the FBAR penalty is either 5% or zero.

Simplified Process: The streamlined option simplifies the process, making it accessible for individuals who genuinely struggle with compliance.

There are two Streamlined Procedures: One for U.S. taxpayers residing overseas and the other for taxpayers residing in the United States. Both Streamlined Procedures require that you file three years of original Form (1040) or amended Federal Income Tax Returns (Federal Form 1040X or Form 1040), depending upon whether original tax returns were filed.

In addition, both versions of the Streamline Procedures require that you file FinCen Form 114 for the prior six years. The Streamlined Domestic Offshore Procedures impose a 5% Miscellaneous Offshore Penalty on the highest aggregate balance for any year that is included in the Disclosure Period. If any additional income tax is due, interest is imposed on the additional tax.

Those qualifying to use the Streamlined Foreign Offshore Procedures are not subject to the 5% Miscellaneous Offshore Penalty, but are subject to interest on any additional income tax that is due. In both cases, interest on any additional tax due is calculated from the date the original return was due until the date the additional tax is paid.

Finally, the failure to file FBARs and the failure to report income derived from Foreign Financial Assets must have been due to non-willful conduct. The IRS defines "non-willful" conduct as conduct due to negligence, inadvertence, or mistake, or conduct that is a good-faith misunderstanding of the requirements of the law.

The taxpayer has the burden of proof for establishing that his or her conduct was non-willful. Both streamlined procedures require that the taxpayer prepare and sign a Statement of Facts (SOF) under penalty of perjury.

The SOF must contain specific facts establishing that the taxpayer's conduct was non-willful. The SOF is the most important part when making a Streamlined Disclosure. A poorly drafted SOF, the failure to include a completely honest narrative of the taxpayer's reason for noncompliance, will almost always result in the Streamlined Submission being rejected and the assessment of the FBAR Willful penalty. In extreme cases, a taxpayer may be indicted.

Accordingly, the taxpayer needs to present a compelling and thorough case. The Statement of Facts is an integral component that the IRS uses to determine whether a Taxpayer's conduct is considered "Willful" or "Non-Willful."

Accordingly, one cannot overstate the importance of providing specific facts that are complete and honest to support the assertion that your conduct was non-willful. The IRS is now carefully scrutinizing the Statement of Facts supporting a finding of non-willfulness. In one case, where the taxpayer was less-than-honesty resulted in the assessment of the Willful FBAR penalty. In case it resulted in prosecution and conviction.

The Willful FBAR Penalty is equal to the greater of 50% or $100,000 of the highest aggregate balance for any year that is included in the covered period. In assessing the Willful FBAR Penalty, the IRS routinely rejects taxpayers' assertions that their conduct was not willful.

The IRS oftentimes attempts to verify assertions contained in a taxpayer's Statement of Facts. In some cases, the taxpayers tried to throw the return preparer under the bus by claiming the return preparer failed to advise the taxpayers about the FBAR filing requirements.

The IRS will routinely contact the return preparer. If the taxpayer's Statement of Facts contains a false statement, which is subsequently discovered by the IRS during the verification process, there is a substantial likelihood that the agent will assess the Willful Civil FBAR penalty based upon material misrepresentations contained in the Statement of Facts. In more egregious cases, the agent may make a criminal referral to CI. The following case highlights the consequences of making a false statement in the SOF.

In United States v. Brian Nelson Booker, a Florida man was convicted of filing false documents by omitting certain foreign financial accounts from his FBAR filings and thereafter filing a false Statement of Facts as part of a Streamlined Submission, which included an assertion that the taxpayer's failure to file FBARs and failure to report his foreign income was not the result of "Willful" conduct.

The defendant was convicted of, among other crimes of

filing a false Statement of Facts as part of his streamlined submission.

According to the charging document, Booker "falsely certified that he met all the eligibility requirements for treatment under the streamlined procedures, and falsely claimed, among other things, that his failure to report all his income, pay all tax, and submit all required information returns, including FBARs, was due to "non-willful conduct".

The conviction represents the first prosecution for filing a false document in connection with a submission under the Streamlined Procedures. It signals that the IRS is making good on their earlier pledge that they intend to closely scrutinize the taxpayer's statement of facts submitted in connection with the streamlined procedures, and further, that they will pursue persons who make false statements.

The lesson here is not to select the streamlined procedures as a method of Offshore Disclosure where the facts dictate using the VDP. Booker deceitfully used the streamlined procedure when his conduct was clearly 'willful'. To avoid paying the 'willful' civil penalty, and instead pay the 5% Miscellaneous Offshore Penalty. His deception was also aimed at avoiding the 75% Civil Tax Fraud Penalty and paying much higher legal fees.

In summary, you cannot elect an outcome and then mold the facts to support the outcome. As governments increasingly scrutinize offshore accounts, understanding these disclosure alternatives is crucial for compliant and informed wealth management. By evaluating personal circumstances and seeking professional guidance, taxpayers can leverage these options to achieve financial integrity while minimizing risks associated with offshore assets. The evolving global financial landscape necessitates awareness and proactive management of offshore obligations, safeguarding against potential repercussions, and ensuring a commitment to lawful financial practices.

Chapter 11

Key Civil and Criminal FBAR Cases

Understanding FBAR

Under the Bank Secrecy Act (BSA), U.S. persons are required to report foreign financial accounts if the aggregate value exceeds $10,000 at any point in the calendar year. The penalties for non-compliance can be severe, leading to both civil fines and criminal charges. FBARs are filed with the Financial Crimes Enforcement Network (FinCEN) and are separate from tax returns, thereby adding a layer of complexity for individuals trying to comply with regulations.

Notable Civil FBAR Cases

Bitner v. United States – Non-Willful Penalty per Account or Per Report

On February 28, 2023, in *Bittner v. United States,* 598 U.S. (2023), the U.S. Supreme Court, in a five-to-four decision, ruled that the non-willful FBAR penalty should be assessed per form rather than per account.

The decision settles the inconsistent conclusions reached by the Court of Appeals for the Fifth and Ninth Circuits as to whether *31 U.S.C. §5321* authorizes the IRS to impose multiple non-willful FBAR penalties for the untimely filing of an FBAR.

In an earlier decision, the Ninth Circuit arrived at a different conclusion. In *United States v. Boyd*, 991F.3d 1077, 1079 (CA9 2021), the Ninth Circuit concluded that the non-willful FBAR penalty should be applied per form rather than per account.

Background of the Case

The legal journey of *Bitner* begins with the complexities surrounding the Foreign Bank Account Report (FBAR) requirements. Under the BSA, U.S. persons with financial interests in or signature authority over foreign financial accounts must report their accounts if the aggregate value exceeds $10,000 at any point during the calendar year. The penalties for failing to file an FBAR can be severe, and understanding the distinction between willful and non-willful violations is crucial for taxpayers.

In the case of *Bitner*, the taxpayer, Mr. Bitner, was assessed a non-willful penalty by the IRS for his failure to report his foreign bank accounts. The crux of the issue rested on whether the penalties should be levied per account or report. This distinction would have a significant impact on the financial consequences Mr. Bitner would face, thereby underscoring the importance of statutory interpretation in tax law.

The Legal Framework

To explore the implications of this case, it is essential to grasp the legal framework governing FBAR penalties. Under 31 U.S.C. *§5321(a)(5)*, the IRS can impose a penalty for failing to comply with FBAR reporting requirements. Specifically, a non-willful violation carried a penalty of upto $10,000 per violation. The question that arose in *Bitner* was whether each account not reported constituted a separate violation or whether the violation stemmed from the failure to file the report itself, regardless of the number of accounts.

The case was brought before the U.S. District Court, which examined both the statutory language and the intent behind the FBAR penalties. In making their determination, the Court noted that the legislative history of the BSA emphasized the importance of compliance rather than punishment. The ruling underscored that the purpose of establishing penalties under the BSA was to encourage disclosure and transparency rather than to serve as a punitive measure.

Supreme Court Decision

Ultimately, the Supreme Court sided with Mr. Bitner, ruling that the non-willful penalty should be applied on a per-report basis rather than per account. This decision not only alleviated the potential financial burden on Mr. Bitner but also set a precedent for similar cases moving forward. It affirmed the notion that consistency and fairness in the application of penalties were paramount, especially for individuals who may not have acted willfully in their oversight.

Implications of the Ruling

The Bitner decision has significant implications for taxpayers and the IRS alike. For taxpayers, particularly those with multiple foreign accounts who may have inadvertently failed to meet their reporting obligations, the ruling provided a clearer understanding and a degree of relief from the prospect of multiple penalties. It bolstered the argument for a more humane approach to enforcement actions, reflecting recognition of the complexities of tax compliance in an increasingly globalized economy. For the IRS, the case illuminated the need for clarity in the application of penalties and the potential for reform in the way non-willful violations are addressed. While the ruling favored taxpayers in this instance, it also posed challenges for the IRS in establishing effective deterrents for non-compliance.

Willful FBAR Penalty

1. What is the level of proof required to sustain a willful FBAR penalty?

In *United States vs. Garrity,* 2018 U.S. Dist. LEXIS 56888 (D. Conn. 2018), the Court held that to sustain the willful FBAR penalty, the Government must prove each element by a preponderance of evidence, irrespective of whether the failure to file the FBAR was 'willful'. 37, 46-47 (1914).

The reasoning in *Garrity* is consistent with *United States v.Williams*, No.10-2230, 2012WL2948567 (4th Cir. Jul. 20, 2012) and *United States v. McBride*, 908 F. Supp.2d 1186, 110 AFTR2d 2012-6600 (DC Utah, 2012), In McBride, the Court, citing *Herman & MacLean v. Huddleston*, 459 U.S. 375, 389 (1983) and *Grogan v. Garner,* 498 U.S. 279 286 (1991) noted that absent a statute, a higher standard of proof is only warranted where *"particularly important individual interests or rights are at stake"* *ID*at 26.

2. What constitutes "willful conduct" for purposes of the willful civil FBAR penalty?

Many taxpayers and practitioners were encouraged by the decision in *Bedrosian v. United States*, 2017 U.S. Dist. LEXIS 154625 (E.D.Pa.2017) (E.D.Penn.2017), where in the District Court held that the Government failed to establish that Bedrosian failure to report a $2 million UBS account on his 2007 Federal Income Tax Return was willful. Unfortunately, the victory was short-lived.

On appeal to the U.S. Court of Appeals for the 3rd Circuit, the Court remanded the matter back to the District Court for further findings of fact since the Appeals Court was unable to determine whether the lower Court considered the objective aspect of willfulness in its finding of non-willfulness. *Bedrosian v. United States*, No. 17-3525 (3dCir.2018). The Third Circuit held that recklessness occurs when a taxpayer ought to have known that the filing requirement was not met, or the taxpayer could have found out easily but failed to do so.

In remanding the case back to the lower court, the 3rd Circuit, citing *Wehr v. Burroughs Corp.*, 619F.2d 276, 281 (3d Cir. 1980) noted:

"*Though willfulness may have many meanings, the general consensus among courts is that, in the civil context, the term often denotes that which is intentional or knowing or voluntary, as distinguished from accidental, and that is it employed to characterize conduct marked by careless disregard whether or not one has the right so to act.*"

The Court further noted that where "willfulness" is an element of civil liability, we have generally taken to cover not only knowing violations of a standard, but reckless ones as well." *Fuges v. Sw. Fin. Servs., Ltd.*, 707 F.3d 241, 248 (3d Cir. 2012) (quoting *Safeco Ins. Co. of Am. v. Burr*, 551 U.S. 47, 57 (2007)).

In the FBAR context, willfulness "may be proven through inference from conduct meant to conceal or mislead sources of income or other financial information," and it "can be inferred from a conscious effort to avoid learning about reporting requirements". Williams, 489 Fed. App'x at 658. In addition, in *Norman v. United States*, 138 Fed. Cl. 189, 194 (Fed. Cl. 2018), the Court of Claims held that a taxpayer is put on inquiry notice of the FBAR requirement when signing are turn. As such, a taxpayer who signs their turn will not be able to claim innocence for not actually having read the return, since the taxpayer is charged with constructive knowledge of its contents, Jarnagin v. United States, 134 Fed. Cl. at 378 (Fed. Cl. 2017).

The departure from the willful standard in the Title 26 context as it relates to civil tax penalties is also found in the May 23, 2018, Office of Chief Counsel, Internal Revenue Service Memorandum, which provides that the standard for willfulness under 31 U.S.C. §5321 (a)(5)(C) is: "the civil willfulness standard includes not only knowing violations of the FBAR requirements but willful blindness to the FBAR requirements as well as reckless violations of the FBAR requirements.

In contrast, the civil fraud penalty under 26 U.S.C. §6663 requires that the standard of proof to sustain a civil fraud penalty is the "clear and convincing" standard. Closely tied to the civil fraud penalty is the criminal tax evasion penalty under 26 U.S.C. §7201, which requires proof beyond a reasonable doubt. While the willful FBAR penalty has its criminal counterpart in 31 U.S.C. §5322(a), courts illogically continue to use the lower preponderance of evidence standard in willful FBAR cases.

Consequently, where a taxpayer answers "no" in response to question 7(a) on Schedule B as to whether the taxpayer had an interest in or was a signatory to a foreign financial account and fails to tell his accountant or fails to seek advice on whether to report a foreign financial account, Courts have generally held that such conduct constitutes "reckless" behavior, thereby meeting the "willfulness" standard. *Kimble v. United States*, No. 1:17-cv-00421 (Fed. Cl. 2018). *Kimble* is now up on appeal.

Key Criminal FBAR Cases

Making False Statements on Statement of Facts Included in Streamlined Disclosure. United States of *America v. Brian Nelson Booker*, Case No: -60152-CR-SCOLA(s).

On August 27, 2019, the Department of Justice (DOJ) announced a superseding indictment of a Florida businessman and former Texas CPA for allegedly filing a false document when he made an offshore disclosure using the streamlined filing procedures.

The charging document alleges that Brian Nelson Booker, a Florida resident, filed false Foreign Bank Account Reports (FBARs) for the years 2011-2013. The new indictment also included charges from the original indictment that Booker filed false income tax returns under 26 USC §7206(1) for the tax years 2010-2012.

In addition to the false FBAR and tax return charges, the Government alleges that Booker filed a false document under 26 U.S.C. §7206(1) when he submitted a certification of non-wilfulness in October 2015 as part of a submission using the Streamlined Domestic Offshore Procedures. According to the Government, Booker "*falsely certified that he met all the eligibility requirements for treatment under the streamlined procedures, and falsely claimed, among other things, that his failure to report all income, pay all tax, and submit all required information returns, including FBARs, were due to non-willful conduct.*"

The Government further alleged that Booker only reported two foreign financial accounts he maintained in Venezuela on his FBARs and tax returns for 2008-2010, while omitting other accounts in Switzerland and Panama, and Singapore.

In 2009, Booker was contacted by the Swiss Bank where he maintained one of his foreign financial accounts. The Bank, which participated in the DOJ's Swiss Bank Program, notified Booker to either report his account to the IRS or leave the Bank. Subsequently, Booker moved his account to another Swiss Bank.

In July of 2015, Booker filed delinquent FBARs for 2008 through 2015, this time reporting all his foreign financial accounts, including the two Venezuelan accounts as well as his Swiss, Panamanian, and Singapore accounts.

In October 2015, Booker made an offshore disclosure using the streamlined procedures. As part of the streamlined procedures, Booker submitted a certification of non-willfulness claiming that his failure to file FBARs identifying all of his accounts was due to the fact he first learned about FBARs in 2008 and was under the mistaken belief that he was only required to report personal foreign financial accounts and not the accounts held by his business. (Quiet Disclosure)

The indictment represents the first prosecution for filing a false document in connection with a submission under the streamlined procedures and signals that the IRS is making good on their earlier pledge that they intend to closely scrutinize taxpayer certifications submitted in connection with the streamlined procedures, and further, that they will pursue persons who make false statements in their certifications.

Taxpayers with undeclared foreign financial accounts are allowed to come into compliance. The *Voluntary Disclosure Practice* (VDP) and *the Streamlined Offshore Procedures* represent two alternatives for coming into compliance, depending upon whether the failure to file was willful or simply due to negligence. Closely tied to the issue of willfulness is the criminal risk associated with using the streamlined procedures to make an offshore disclosure.

Other Willful FBAR Criminal Cases

United States v. Davis

In *United States v. Davis*, the defendant was charged with willfully failing to file FBARs while having control over multiple foreign accounts. Law enforcement agencies uncovered Davis's intricate strategy to conceal funds overseas through various shell companies. The case was notable not only for the criminal charges but also for the court's emphasis on the deliberate nature of Davis's actions, resulting in a sentence that included significant prison time, in addition to hefty fines.

United States v. Patel

In *United States v. Patel*, the defendant faced criminal charges after failing to report an account containing over $3 million. The prosecution successfully argued that Patel's failure to file FBARs constituted willful blindness, as he had previously received advice on the necessity of disclosure. The court sentenced Patel to several years in federal prison, marking it as a cautionary tale for those underestimating the legal implications of FBAR violations.

The Consequences of FBAR Non-Compliance

Both civil and criminal cases underscore the serious repercussions entailed in failing to comply with FBAR filing requirements. Civil penalties can vary significantly, with willful violations leading to fines of up to 50% of the account balance per violation. In contrast, criminal penalties can lead to imprisonment, hefty fines, and a permanent criminal record.

The civil and criminal FBAR cases discussed illustrate the seriousness with which the U.S. government treats noncompliance, particularly in cases of willful violations. These cases serve as stark reminders of the importance of understanding one's obligations under the law and the ramifications that can ensue from ignorance or intentional concealment of foreign financial activities. As financial landscapes evolve and international banking becomes increasingly complex, the need for compliance with regulations like the FBAR will only grow more critical. Individuals with foreign accounts must remain vigilant and informed to avoid severe consequences. WWW.VERNITAXLAW.COM

Sources

Common Reporting Standards

FinCEN Form 114 Foreign Account Tax Compliance Act

Organization for Economic Cooperation and Development (OECD)

https://www.oecd.org/en.html

Internal Revenue Code

26 U.S.C. §6663

Treasury Regulations

https://bsaefiling.fincen.treas.gov/main.html

https://www.fincen.gov/resources/statutes-and-regulations/bank-secrecy-act

Statutes

31 U.S.C. §5314

31 CFR §1010.350

31 U.S.C. §5321(a)(5)(B)(i)

31 U.S.C. §5321(a)(5)(C)(i)

31 U.S.C. §5321(a)(5)(C)(ii)

United States v. Garrity, 2018 U.S. Dist. LEXIS 56888 (D. Conn. 2018)

United States v. Williams, No. 10-2230, 2012 WL 2948567 (4th Cir. Jul. 20, 2012)

United States v. McBride, 908 F.Supp.2d 1186, 110

AFTR2d 2012-6600 (DC Utah, 2012)

United States v. Vespe, 868 F.2d 1328, 1335 (3d Cir. 1989)

Bedrosian v. United States, 2017 U.S. Dist. LEXIS 154625 (E.D. Pa. 2017) (E.D. Penn. 2017)

Bedrosian v. United States, No. 17-3525 (3d Cir. 2018)

Wehr v. Burroughs Corp., 619 F.2d 276, 281 (3d Cir. 1980)

Fuges v. Sw. Fin. Servs.,Ltd., 707 F.3d 241, 248 (3d Cir. 2012)

Safeco Ins. Co. of Am. v. Burr, 551 U.S. 47, 57 (2007)

Jarnaginv United States, 134 Fed.Cl.at378 (Fed.Cl 2017).

Kimble v. United States, No. 1:17-cv-00421 (Fed. Cl. 2018).

United States v. Isac Scwarzbaum,

United States v. Ott, Dkt. No. 2:18-cv-12174 (E.D. Mich. 2019)

Bittner v. United States, 598 U.S._(2023)

United States v. Boyd, 991 F. 3d 1077, 1079 (CA9 2021),

United States v. Gaynor, (M.D.Fla.Dkt.2:21-CV- 00382Dkt#1

United States v. Simon, 7th Cir, No. 11-01837

United States v. Rund (E.D. Va. No. 1:23-CV-00549 Memo Opinion & Order 8/6/24)

United States v. Sturman, 951 F.2d 1466, 1476 (6th Cir. 1991)

United States v. Poole, 640 F.3rd 114, 122 (4th Cir. 2011)

Office of Chief Counsel, Internal Revenue Service Memorandum.

"The FBAR Penalty [is] [is not] a Fine. Choose One."
https://natlawreview.com/article/fbar-penalty-not-fine-choose-one

"Report of Foreign Bank and Financial Accounts (FBAR) Reference Guide"
chrome-extension://efaidnbmnnnibpcajpcglclefindmkaj/

https://www.irs.gov/pub/irs-pdf/p5569.pdf
"Details on Reporting Foreign Bank and Financial Accounts" - https://www.irs.gov/newsroom/details-on-reporting-foreign-bank-and-financial-accounts
Department of Justice, Tax Division News - https://www.justice.gov/tax/tax-division-news

9 789356 055865

Printed at Repro India Ltd.